Arf Angels
and Other
Heavenly Creatures

———

True Stories
of
Animal Visitations

Written and Edited by

Anita Perry

ISBN: 0-7596-5436-0

This book is printed on acid free paper.

Printed in the United States of America

Front cover photo by Ruth Hiestand.

1stBooks - rev. 3/14/02

This book is dedicated to Barney who started it all, to the storytellers who shared their experiences, to each and every one of their beloved pets, and to all of God's creatures.

To Susan Perry, my daughter, who seemed to be dressed in Velcro and the stray animals that stuck to her as she made her way home from school and work.

Susan designed the back cover, acted as editor and spent countless hours on the computer. Thank you, Susan, for your dedication and just for being the person you are.

Published by: 1ˢᵗ Books Library
A Division of Advance Marketing Technologies, L.L.C.
www.1stBooks.com

Animal groups who wish to use this book as a fundraiser
may purchase it at a discount at
ArfAngels.net.

Contents

Introduction

As you read the case histories presented in this book, you may agree that each pet was instrumental in providing an opportunity for change and acted as an enhancement or sometimes a catalyst to their people's spiritual growth. After the death of a pet, many owners change their whole perspective as to the importance of sharing their lives with an animal.

When I was eight or nine years old, I wanted a pet so badly. Money was scarce at the time, and I suppose that would have been an additional, expensive burden on my family's budget.

One summer day, I decided that, on my own, I would get a pet anyway and hide it from my family. I sneaked a very long string from the cupboard drawer to act as a leash for my new pet. Then I started my search. I wasn't allowed to leave the yard, so I was a bit limited. Quite some time into this "safari," I saw a very large beetle. He, surely, couldn't eat very much. He would have to do. I tied the string to one leg and proceeded to take "Linden" for a walk. After a couple of steps and a bit of resistance, he began to fly. That wasn't in my plan. We toured the yard a few times. This wasn't going to work. He didn't like to be petted, and I knew my Mom wouldn't allow him to sleep on my bed. I untied his leash and set Linden free. He hadn't fulfilled my need for a pet anyway.

Pets were not in my life until after I was married. My ex-husband left me a legacy of two wonderful daughters and an introduction to the wonders of animals. For this, I am grateful.

My friend, Ruth, and I were in the habit of bringing so many strays home, he accused me of driving around with meat and the car door open in order to lure dogs into the car. When they were brought home, we managed to locate their owners or find them a good home.

Our daughters also shared a love of animals. When my daughter, Susan, was in high school, she heard of a litter of puppies who were to be destroyed at birth. She asked if we could take them if she could get permission from the dog's caretaker. (The owners were away on vacation.) Of course, we said yes. When the puppies were four days old, Susan brought them home. We all took four-hour shifts around the clock in order to bottle feed them. Even after being taken from their mother at such a young age, we didn't lose any of them. They all thrived.

I didn't dare name them. Had I done so, I wouldn't have been able to part with any of them. Each prospective owner was interviewed, actually grilled, and not all of them passed muster. Those, who did, agreed to give them the necessary shots and have them spayed or neutered. It was also agreed that we could visit them after a year's time. When each puppy left the house, at the age of two months, I was in tears. It was awfully hard to let them go. I wanted to keep all of them. The problem was that we already had three small dogs, and in my area, if you have more than three it is considered a kennel and must be licensed as such.

One special female stole my heart, and I called her Little Brown One. (Not an *official* name.) At the end of a year, we visited them all. When we arrived at Little Brown One's house, the family was just driving into their driveway. I was about 75 feet from the front door of their house, and I waited until they were ready to enter their home. I got out of the car. When the family opened their door, Little Brown One raced past them and, at top speed, leaped into my arms. I wasn't expecting that and reeled back a bit but was able to maintain my balance. The family was puzzled by her behavior and said she had never acted that way before. She stayed next to me for the entire visit. When it was time to go, I shed some more tears and hated to leave her behind.

How could she have remembered and recognized me? She couldn't get my scent from inside the closed house and from that distance. There has to be a bond, or some special unspoken communication that takes place, that is unrecognized or not fully understood at this time, at least by humans.

I feel all the animals that have shared my life have left me a legacy. They demonstrated the meaning of unconditional love, compassion, acceptance, and loyalty. They have helped me grow as a person and have enhanced any good qualities I may have. Perhaps, they helped hone my positive attributes much faster than if I were left to learn these lessons on my own. After each of my pets' deaths, I was better able to face my own mortality and open my mind to things that are spiritual. They were all excellent teachers.

The contributors to this book have all experienced some form of communication with their deceased pets. Some pets came in a dream or vision. Others returned in a more profound manner. Some owners would get just a brief glance, hear their familiar sound, smell their fur, or have a sense of their pet in the room. It could be described as similar to the feeling of someone staring at you, yet no one is physically there.

Before my dog, Barney, died, I had not experienced the return of any of my other beloved pets. Maybe, I hadn't listened or paid attention to what was going on. If something did happen, perhaps, I trivialized it to explain it away or deny it entirely.

Sandy, one of the contributors to this book, summed it up nicely and cited a quote attributed to Angela Monet: "Those who danced were thought to be quite insane by those who could not hear the music."

Are you a dancer or a listener? It is my hope that you are both. If you are not, strive to be. Your own Arf Angel or Heavenly Creature may help show you the way.

It isn't a surprise that we don't hear about deceased pets' souls, or spirits, remaining behind or staying on for a while after their death. This is a subject that is rarely talked about. It might be mentioned to an extremely close and accepting friend, but I have yet to hear it brought up in a conversation or even freely discussed within a family.

My own experience was difficult to talk about, as I feared someone might think I was a bit unstable and unable to cope with the loss of my dear pet, Barney. After several months of feeling him bump against the side of the bed, as he did to get my attention, I told my daughter, Susan, what was happening. She was very supportive and open to any and all possibilities about what was going on.

When I asked a veterinarian if he had heard of this type of phenomenon, he said he certainly had, but that it isn't much talked about. It was at that time, I decided to do research on the subject. Most often, the people who related their stories to me requested anonymity. Their reaction was much the same as mine. Who wants to be labeled as a kook or risk being ridiculed?

It is hoped, as you read this collection of stories, you will find that, indeed, your feelings are validated if you have had a similar experience. Your heart may be warmed and your soul inflamed as you read what others have shared. You may find a smile, a laugh, but expect a few tears as well.

Most of these stories were typed through a few tears, which blurred my view. I feel each story can teach about love, respect, trust, faith, and compassion.

Why don't we experience the return of all our deceased pets? I haven't an explanation. In my case, I feel that each pet I owned helped me evolve spiritually and be more accepting and ready for the experience when it did happen. Whatever the reason for Barney's return, I am eternally grateful.

Over the Rainbow

You will find references to Rainbow Bridge as you read some of the stories. The Rainbow Bridge is that special place where, many feel, our precious pets wait for us to meet them.

Rainbow Bridge

Just this side of heaven is a place called Rainbow Bridge.

When an animal dies that has been especially close to someone here, that pet goes to Rainbow Bridge.

There are meadows and hills for all of our special friends so they can run and play together.

There is plenty of food, water and sunshine, and our friends are warm and comfortable.

All the animals who had been ill and old are restored to health and vigor; those who were hurt or maimed are made whole again, just as we remember them in our dreams of days gone by.

The animals are happy and content, except for one small thing; they miss someone very special to them, who had to be left behind.

They all run and play together, but the day comes when one suddenly stops and looks into the distance. His bright eyes are intent:

His eager body quivers. Suddenly he begins to run from the group, flying over the green grass, his legs carrying him faster and faster.

You have been spotted and when you and your special friend finally meet, you cling together in joyous reunion, never to be parted again. The happy kisses rain upon your face: your hands again caress the beloved head, and you look once more into the trusting eyes of your pet, so long gone from your life but never absent from your heart.

Author Unknown

Barney

Barney came to my home on July 4th at the age of two months. The arrival date was appropriate as his energy level gave new meaning to the Big Bang Theory.

He was destined to stay for almost 17 years, but he continues to remain even after his death.

My daughter, Susan, adopted Barney's mother, Daisey, from a local pound. She looked like a Bearded Collie with long white hair and a few black spots. She had a gentle and sweet nature. It wasn't known at the time of her adoption that she was "with puppies" and later proceeded to give birth to nine. All of them were black and white with the exception of Barney, who was brown and white, and one female with long white hair. Good homes were found for all. My granddaughter, Krissy, pleaded with me to take Barney when I really wanted a black and white female. What was a grandmother to do other than take him?

A short time after his arrival, he developed an appetite for wood, French bread, onions, tissues, paper money, and plastic. He was fed only a commercial kibble, never people food, but when I chopped onions or sliced French bread, I would "accidentally" drop some on the floor. (I later learned that onion is not good for dogs.) He quickly learned that "oops" meant he was getting a goodie.

One day I carelessly dropped the end of a French bread loaf. He gulped it down and began to scratch at his throat. I noticed he seemed to be having trouble breathing, and I panicked. Fortunately, my daughter was there and she gave him the Heimlich maneuver, and the bread popped out. Thereafter, all the crusts were removed from small bite-sized pieces of bread.

Gardening is a favorite pastime for me, and we spent many pleasant times in the garden. There were some curious goings on in the vegetable area. Many of the onions were disappearing. I attributed it to raccoons or opossums that often came into the yard at night. One day while grooming Barney, I got a whiff of onion breath! Mystery solved. Onions always remained a favorite tidbit.

Plastic was a gourmet specialty, which included eyeglass frames, hearing aids, and plastic eating utensils. When Barney developed a more sophisticated palate, he stopped chewing wood, but his appetite for plastic and onions stayed with him for life.

Plastic flowerpots were one of his favorite toys. He would dump the flowers and throw the pots up in the air and chase them. I gave him a Frisbee to toss around, but he preferred the flowerpots. My garden suffered, but eventually I learned to set aside a few empty pots for him.

Until Barney had obedience training, he was kept in the kitchen behind a mesh gate during the night and when I was out of the house. He was content as long as he could see what was going on. His large wicker bed was lined with a king-size bedspread. This proved to be his security blanket, and when he had the run of the house, he dragged it with him wherever he went. This made it difficult for me to maneuver around him. Each week I would cut off a bit of it until it got to be a manageable size. Barney didn't mind as long as he had a piece of it in his mouth. Even when asleep, he had to have a small corner of it in his mouth; this did nothing to further his macho image.

At the age of six months, I took him for obedience training. During this time, I injured my arm, and it was necessary for my granddaughter, Kristin, to work with him at class. He soon learned that home was for fun, but class was serious business.

On graduation day, a professional judge was brought in, and he was top dog of the class. Much to my surprise, he had an almost perfect score. He had one point taken off because he moved his right front foot a fraction of an inch.

This energetic creature could be exasperating at times, but he also had a lot of entertainment value. I adored him. Whenever he got into mischief, I would usually tell him, "Good thing you're cute!"

One evening, my granddaughter and I were out of the house for a couple of hours. When the car pulled into the driveway, we heard a series of yelps and knew that Barney was in pain. Upon entering the house, we saw that his ID tag was caught in the mesh of the gate and kept him in a semi-standing position. A quick trip to the emergency clinic for x-rays and an examination showed a damaged disc. This was to be a problem for the rest of his life, but his joy remained.

Thereafter, he had free run of the house, and his ID and rabies tags were riveted directly onto his collar. They no longer dangled and could not catch on anything.

All the previous dogs that I have had were 12 pounds or under. I enjoyed having them on my lap. I considered Barney a big dog, even though he weighed only 26 pounds. He just didn't fit on my lap, but he would lean against my legs for long periods of time for daily back and joint massages.

Around the age of ten, Barney developed a bit of arthritis. His vet suggested that his bed should be made of three layers of egg-crate foam; this eased the pressure on his hips and back. I had to put two beds in his favorite places, so he wouldn't drag them around from place to place for a nap as he did with his blanket. He continued to play as before but napped more often.

As Barney grew a bit older, his eyes developed some cloudiness, and his hearing was less acute. His strength was affected also. He became more and more attached to me as those problems worsened. If I left the room, he followed. He acted as though he had been trained as a Seeing-Eye-Dog for the visually handicapped. Actually, I was his "Seeing-Person."

Around the age of 12, Barney developed a disease called Cushing's Syndrome, often caused by a growth on the adrenal cortex. For about two days, Barney was not interested in food and just lay quietly. This was so out of character for him that I called his vet to make a house call. After two blood work-ups, a few hours apart, the diagnosis was made. Medication was found to help the condition by making the adrenals inactive. A couple of days later, he was his old self, much to the vet's surprise. He felt that Barney might live a year. Little did he know my Barney.

Barney developed some questionable habits that were cute but at times embarrassing. Remember, he is handsome, friendly, loveable, and a dip. Dip, as in pickpocket. Two times a week, we played bridge at my home. As each person arrived, Barney's sensitive nose alerted him as to who had the most mints, plastic writing pens, credit cards, candy, gum, tissues, and paper money. Once we were deep into the game, he would silently make his way to the most productive handbags, jackets or sweaters. He was very adept at sneaking the treasures that were at hand and could pickpocket at random. I don't know why he had a fascination for credit cards, as he was never allowed to leave home. Of course, he looked forward to bridge days.

He developed a loss of muscle strength towards the end of his life. If he fell, he had to be lifted to a standing or a sitting position. All bare floors were covered for better traction, and it did help. It was still necessary to be with him all the time. When he went outside, I slipped a soft rubber strap under his hips to prevent him from falling. It was both a support to prevent falling and a guide. This seemed to be OK with him. He continued to eat with gusto and retained his will to live. However, the time did come when he didn't want to eat.

In the past, when his nails were clipped, he would receive a kibble treat after each snip. When he reached the point of not eating, I would clip a nail and then give him several pieces of kibble. This ruse worked for a while, and I realized that I was selfish to continue this charade. He chose not to eat, and I knew that his time had come, so I made the appointment for euthanasia. My fear was in doing it too soon — or too late. The veterinarian gave him a tranquilizer, and I was able to hold and cuddle him in my lap for the first time. He was very calm and content lying across my lap and finally fell into a deep sleep.

As I held and rocked him, I felt a strong sense of peace. Barney, the dog who had always held onto life, went gently. I made arrangements for him to be cremated, and his ashes were returned a few days later.

When is the right time to stop trying to save your pet? Deciding to quit can be contrary to your natural instincts. When their quality of life is poor or painful and has no reasonable hope of improving, it is time. You need to decide what is best for **them**. It is always difficult to judge, but it is always important to love them enough to let them go. Hanging on too long only hurts the one you love, and that is the last thing you want to do.

The next while was a very difficult time, and I needed to remind myself that he had completed his allotted time. I was fortunate to have had his companionship for almost 17 years. During that time, Barney taught me the full and true meaning of love, acceptance, and compassion. Had I not been a slow learner, his stay with me may have been shorter.

After his ashes were returned, I placed the small wooden urn on my bedside table until I decided on a proper place to keep them.

A few nights later, I became aware of a small and gentle bump against the side of my bed. My first thought was that it was an earthquake but none were reported on the news the next morning. I then knew that it was Barney telling me that he was still there for me. Such loyalty. This continued for several months on a nightly basis. This had always been the way he asked to go outside during the night or when he wanted attention. When he bumped the bed, I would reach down and pet him or give him a massage. Perhaps, this is what he wanted after his death.

After about three months, I finally asked a vet if he had heard of this type of phenomena, and much to my surprise, he said he had, but it wasn't much talked about. Even if he had not said that, I would have continued to believe that it really was Barney.

One day I decided that I would move his ashes to the bottom drawer of my bedside table. He would still be close to me. Later that night, there was very aggressive bumping against the bed, and I awakened with a start. My daughter had been ill and would come into my room and push against the bed to awaken me so I could help her. I quickly sat up in bed, and my daughter wasn't there. At that point, I felt it had to be an intruder, and I was really frightened. I lay back down and was very still, pretended to be asleep, and listened for sounds to locate where the intruder might be. After quite some time, I realized an intruder wouldn't just wake me up and then leave.

I puzzled over this the next day, and finally came to the conclusion that the only thing different was that I had moved Barney's ashes. He must have had strong feelings about the new location. Needless to say, his ashes are back on top of the nightstand, where they will remain. Thereafter, his bumping against the bed was gentle as before.

I dearly loved all the many animals I have had during my life, but I never had an experience where their spirits had returned. Why would it be different with Barney? I have no explanation for this, and I finally decided that I didn't need one. I just accepted it.

Perhaps, this is just another, more advanced, facet of communication that exists between an owner and his pet. Both Barney and I could read each other quite well.

Immediately after Barney's death, his food and medications were donated to a shelter. It took a great while longer, several months really, before I was able to remove his nose prints from a mirrored closet door near his bed. I wanted so much to keep a part of him with me. I was forced to be satisfied with the little teeth marks on the side of a kitchen cupboard that he put there in his puppyhood. Yes, he was a joy in my life, and I will always be thankful that he raced through his life, and mine, with such great abandon.

Anita Perry

Bear

My mother died when I was 21. In order to put some love into my life, I adopted Bear, a black Labrador Retriever. She was the spunkiest pup in her litter. She was my chosen one, but I was disappointed to see that she was wearing a marked collar. I thought it meant she had already been selected. I said that she was the puppy that I had to have and offered more money than the normal fee. The breeder told me she was not for sale because she had suffered a seizure. I was drawn to this pup and she to me. She wouldn't leave my side, so the owners gave her to me free. This was done with the understanding that she had no guarantee and would not be used for breeding. No problem there. She was my Bear.

My spunky Bear turned into my greatest joy. I missed my mom so much, and it was Bear that made me smile. She was far from perfect. She ate walls, furniture, floors; you name it. She was so smart; she learned obedience commands in just a few days.

She was an angel when I was home, but when she was bored it was quite a different story. She just loved mischief. One day when I returned from work, I opened the door and found all 90 pounds of her fast asleep on the kitchen table. I still laugh about it.

Bear had an uncanny knack for reading my moods. When I was sick in bed, she was beside herself. She first offered her bone to me and insisted I keep it. When that didn't work, she looked for something else. She spent the better part of an hour bringing me everything she loved in order to make me feel better. By this time, the bed was filled with toys. She was trying so hard to make me happy, so I got up and pretended she had cured me.

I feel, we were meant to be together. She was my best friend and had a definite purpose in my life. She helped me deal with my mother's death, and I credit her with saving my life.

I spent four years in a very abusive relationship. I lived with a police officer and felt it would be useless to report the abuse. How could I call the cops when he was one? There were many times he put a gun to my head during a drunken rage. I accepted the abuse and didn't have the courage to leave.

During one rage, Bear stepped in and took a punch to the snout. That was the first time he hit Bear, and that was the last time he touched either of us. I took my dog and left my own home. The next two weeks were spent running from friend to friend. Finally, he realized the relationship was over, and I was able to move back home. Now I was strong enough to go to his chief, and animal welfare as well, to report the abuse. I find it ironic that I could act because he hit my Bear. She made me realize my life was really worthwhile. Thanks to Bear, I saw the light.

With that part of our lives behind us, we settled in to many happy times. We spent days in the park, visited friends, and played at every opportunity.

It was during this time that I began to rescue barn kitties. I saved about thirty, and Bear loved all of them. She had great mothering instincts. One day I brought home a very special rescue. It was a beautiful little Birman female. While I was waiting for the right home placement, Bear decided she was her cat. I named her Fancy. This rounded out our family nicely.

I always had it in the back of my mind that Bear's time with me would be short. She remained healthy with the exception of two more seizures at the ages of one and four.

Bear was a little slow getting up one morning. I looked at her back leg and noticed it was swollen. The swelling reached up as far as her back nipple. I took her to the vet and was happy to hear that it was only an infection. Some antibiotics and anti-inflammatory drugs would soon have her back to her old self. The very next day, I saw an improvement. Thank God! I couldn't lose my Bear.

That happy day was a Wednesday, but it didn't last long. Friday morning Bear was down. Overnight her whole side had swollen so badly, I had to carry this 90-pound loving creature to the vet's office. The doctor took another fluid sample and came back to tell me how sorry he was. It was an aggressive form of cancer, and her body was shutting down. There was no hope for her, and I had to put her to rest.

Bear was such a special dog, the doctor took the time to write me a two page letter about her. Her life ended just short of eight years. Sometimes I think she waited until I got my life back on track, and then her job was done.

Her visit to me came one week after she left me. It took me a week to put her food and water dishes away and vacuum away her fur. That night I heard the old familiar sound of the toilet seat being lifted and then crash down. It had been Bear's way of telling me, "Mom, ya better change my water dish, or I'm going to drink out of the toilet." She had done that for years. I put her water bowl back out for the cat to use. Her visit left me feeling sad but calm.

Bear's second visit came about one month after she died. My room was chilly, but I didn't want to turn the heat on so early in the season. I just bundled up and went to bed. In the middle of the night, I felt her body warming my back where she always lay. I wasn't dreaming. She was really there, and I was tempted to feel her "spot" to see if it was warm too. I didn't because I knew that warmth was only for me.

Bear's last visit was to see her buddy, Fancy, the Birman cat that she loved so dearly. Fancy had this strange, loud purr that she only used when she was lying with Bear. She had done it since she was little and stopped doing it the day Bear died. I thought I would never hear that purr again.

Fancy was in her usual spot on my pillow when she jumped down, and ran, to the place where Bear always slept when she wasn't on the bed. She flopped down and began to purr. This prissy cat does not flop down for anything! After this incident, I never heard that purr again. I felt that strange calm feeling again as I did after the previous two visits. I was pleased that Fancy also knew that Bear was with us.

I haven't heard from Bear since then, at least I think not. I am a little suspicious that she came to see my new dog, a gray rescue, named Blue. Blue would not touch any of Bear's toys until the day I came home after a terrible day at work. That afternoon, Blue took Bear's toys out of the basket and has played with them ever since. I felt that familiar calm. I can't be sure if it was just the idea of Blue and Bear sharing toys or if she was really there. Maybe, if Bear comes home again, she will tell me.

Alisa P.

Shadow

Shadow got her name, not from her black and white coloring, but from her size. I used to tell her she wasn't even the shadow of a dog, and the name stuck; therefore, the name Evening Shadow went on her AKC papers.

She came from the first litter of Chihuahuas that I bred. She was the runt of the litter, only about two-thirds the size of the other three pups, when she was born. She probably never weighed more than three-and-a-half pounds in her life. She was so tiny and unfinished at birth, I delayed registering the pups because I felt she wouldn't make it. I bought formula because I expected to hand feed her. She was a fighter from the beginning. She was an expert at nudging out the bigger pups at the dinner table, and I never had to use that formula. Nobody pushed her around. She ended up an intriguing combination of alpha-pup and runt. I was going to keep one pup from the litter, and had already selected her sister, Ginnie, but I grew to respect this little scrap of a dog so much that I ended up keeping both females.

Just by looking at the expression on her little black face, you knew she was trouble. She was the first to learn and accept new things and was generally at the bottom of any and all mischief. She was never much for playing with toys, though she did especially like rawhide shoes. She loved to take them apart. Shadow and her sister, Ginnie, were inseparable playmates. In fact, when Ginnie finally had her first litter of pups, Shadow was so upset that she went on an eight-day hunger strike. Ultimately, of course, she accepted the pups, learned to play with them, and became Aunt Shaddie, the pup-sitter, for subsequent litters.

She displayed incredible reasoning ability for a dog. I used to tell people she wasn't really a dog but a reincarnated person. She played practical jokes on her sister ... not accidents; she discovered what would work and then used it time after time. Her favorite trick was "hide the treat." When the dogs came in from outside, they always got a treat. The others would gulp theirs down, but Shadow would sometimes hold her treat in her mouth. When the others were finished, she would make a big production of burying her treat under her blanket. Ginnie would wait impatiently until she was finished, then go and dig there to find it. When she couldn't find it, she would look at Shadow, who was sitting a few feet away watching. At this point, Shadow would drop it from her mouth and finally eat it. Poor Ginnie fell for it every time.

Shadow feared nothing. She was a very social dog ... loved people and other dogs, as long as they weren't too much bigger than she was. Early on she decided that she was my dog, and her name became appropriate in another way because she was literally my shadow. She made it very clear, while she loved other people just fine, I belonged to her.

When she was eight years old, she developed heart trouble and was on medication for what would be nearly seven more years. At 12, she contracted some nameless virus that put her close to death. The vet recommended that it might be time to put her to sleep. I couldn't quite do it then, and it turned out well. She suddenly decided that she was going to live and did so for nearly three more years.

Shadow was the first dog I had to choose to put to sleep. This occurred when she was almost 15, in February of 1992. Her body was shutting down. She was suffering from kidney failure and anoxia, but her fighting spirit just wouldn't give up.

That last visit to see the vet was so difficult. I wanted to take her back home in hopes that she would rally again as she had three years before. That was not to be. I stayed to talk and comfort her as she began her last journey.

I fell into a deep depression and felt full of guilt as well as self-condemnation because I had killed my dog. My two other dogs, Romi and her daughter, Kaylee, couldn't provide the comfort I needed. Kaylee still slept with me but carefully avoided Shadow's place on the bed.

One night I woke up in the pre-dawn hours when it was barely beginning to get light. I looked down to the foot of the bed, and Shadow was there. I could feel her, just a little warm weight, on top of the blanket. Kaylee was there with her, and Shadow was cleaning Kaylee's ears, as she'd always loved to do. Then she looked up at me and wagged her tail, and it was if she were telling me, "It's OK. I'm fine. I'm well and happy now. You did the right thing, so don't feel sad." Shadow slowly faded from view.

Kaylee then came and lay down beside me in the place that used to be Shadow's. She had avoided that spot until that moment ... Kaylee gave me a kiss as if to say, "I'm your dog now. Shadow said that it is OK." I felt comforted and went back to sleep. When morning came, Kaylee was curled up in Shadow's place, and I knew it had not been a dream.

Dee

Kaylee

It seems only a short time passed after Kaylee took her new place on the bed, formerly Shadow's place, that she also left me. (Shadow is in the previous story.) Kaylee began to show signs of kidney failure. I couldn't bear the thought of her leaving me so soon after Shadow's death.

I had a lengthy talk with the vet about her situation. I didn't want to make another decision, to let another pet go, and asked him about letting her die at home when it was her time. The vet explained to me what was happening to her body, how she was feeling, and how much she would suffer before death took her. I knew I couldn't allow her to go through that much pain.

My heart was so heavy, but I managed to face the situation. I held her close to me and told her I was letting her go to be with her mother, Romi, and Shadow, and Ginnie. She gave me a tiny kiss, and I felt she understood. It was her way of thanking me for letting her go.

I feel that this is a caring thing that we can do for our beloved pets. When there is no hope, we must end their suffering. I guess we can debate forever about man and nature. Often men set themselves above nature, and that, I feel, is unnatural. I needed to make the decision about Kaylee from a humane standpoint. I would only hope that someday we would become civilized enough to allow our fellow humans the right to die as well.

A short while after Kaylee died, I went through a particularly difficult time. There were too many upsets, over which, I felt I had no control. I found that I missed Kaylee and all my other Rainbow-Bridge-babies even more than usual.

One afternoon when I was feeling especially sorry for my self, I heard a loud rumble of thunder. The sun was shining, and there were no signs of an approaching storm. I looked outside and saw the most magnificent rainbow. It stretched all the way from end to end — the most beautiful rainbow I've ever seen. For some reason, something compelled me to say, "Hi Kaylee." Then I had a beautiful feeling of peace come over me. I felt that Kaylee was telling me, "Hey Mom, I'm fine, and I'm here. We're all here. This is where we live now. We love you, and we're waiting for you." I could only stand, and stare, and let the feeling of peace wash over me as I watched the rainbow slowly fade away.

Now, when things are difficult, I remember that feeling, and I can handle it better now. I know Rainbow Bridge is real ... I've seen it.

A couple of days after Kaylee's death, I saw her trotting from the bathroom to the bedroom ... just a glimpse of chocolate and white fur. That reinforced my feeling that our pets remain with us, at least, for a period of time. Knowing that Shadow and Kaylee are together gives me peace.

Dee

Hondo

I went to the grocery store for bread and milk. I returned home with bread, milk, and a cat. There were two small boys in the Lucky parking lot holding a box of kittens. I stopped to look and saw that one was black with a small white spot on his cheek, a white belly, and four white feet. He was longhaired and handsome. He had the most enormous white whiskers I had ever seen, and there was just something about him that I couldn't resist. The boys told me, "We can't go home until we give them away."

I am allergic to cats, and having him adopt me was not something planned but a match made in cat-dom. I named him Hondo, after the title character from Louis L'Amour's first novel. It suited him just fine.

We already had two dogs, Maggie, a black Lab, and Max, who was a black and white Cocker Spaniel. They took to the kitten in very different ways. Maggie ignored him, after some initial interest, while Max became a surrogate parent. Hondo had a nightly bath supplied by the dutiful spaniel. They slept and ate together.

His favorite playthings were a ball, wrapping paper, and paper bags. Any folded bag left on the floor immediately became his perch. Like most cats, he couldn't resist sitting right in the middle of anything unusual that was available. He never bothered my annual Christmas tree, never attempted to climb it, but always liked to sleep beneath it and drink out of the water reservoir.

Hondo never drank out of the water bowl I kept in the house. He drank out of the birdbath, standing to his full height, and looked like a little man. He grew to be a "big guy," long, lean, and about 12 pounds. Hondo didn't like having his whiskers crowded by anything. His food bowls were vintage American dinnerware called nappies. They were shallow and wide enough to accommodate those long whiskers.

I am pretty much a dog person, so I trained Hondo the same way I trained my dogs. A helpful veterinarian taught me how to discipline him, in a non-violent fashion to which he responded. Hondo quickly learned to come when he was called, stay off tables, counters, and furniture.

We installed a doggy door. Hondo began spending most of his time outside, mostly in our yard but also across the street, where our neighbor has several acres of land. He became a "wild soul," as many cats can be, but continued to sleep inside and come when called. Often in the wee hours, he went on hunting trips. He brought his "trophies" back to Max. Hondo loved the outside, the rain, the wind, and even the heat in summer.

The minute I woke, even without making a noise, he would meow to me, jump off the fence, and come inside for a morning ear scratch.

When he was about four, our Max died, and Hondo became much more solitary. Three years after that, we lost Maggie too, and although we had two other dogs by this time, Hondo was never quite the same.

As it happens with many outdoor cats, a car killed Hondo when he was almost ten years old. It was a rainy night, before Thanksgiving, when a neighbor found him on the sidewalk.

Now it is a year later. We miss him terribly, although he is still in our hearts. I suppose that he is not quite ready to go because my husband and I often hear the unique noise he made when jumping off the fence. He had a quiet, furtive way of coming through the pet doors; and even now, while our three dogs are asleep, I hear the soft flop of the doors. We hear him often on windless nights and early mornings.

We had never had the experience of having a beloved pet return to us. Perhaps, this time we were more receptive. If it had happened before, maybe we weren't ready. Whatever the reason, we are comforted that his spirit is here.

Christine Harrison

Ginger

Ginger, our Golden Retriever, was such a sweet dog. She was with us for almost 12 years. We liked the qualities of this breed and searched for that "special one."

Just before my husband and I bought Ginger, we had purchased another Golden from a breeder and named her Shannon. This was a special name to us. Had we had a daughter, that would have been her name.

When Shannon was brought home, she seemed very quiet and docile for a puppy. It was during this time that the disease, parvo, was rampant. We immediately took her to the vet, but he was unable to save her. We only had her for four traumatic days.

Shortly after that, we found Ginger. There was another female that tugged at our hearts, but we finally decided on Ginger.

A few days later, the breeder called and asked about our new puppy's health, and we were pleased to tell her that she was doing beautifully. We were then told that the other little female had also gotten parvo. We felt badly, but believed we were destined to have Ginger all along.

We had two small sons who were very active in soccer. Ginger aspired to be a team player as well. As a result, we went through a few balls. She held them so tightly in her mouth that her teeth would puncture them.

Exercise was never a problem. Ryan, our youngest son, would ride his bicycle around and around the block, and Ginger happily ran alongside. It was such a warming sight to see the two of them, a happy boy and his dog.

Ginger was very protective of our sons and neighborhood children as well. There were neighbor kids who lived across the street, and one day a brother and sister got into a little spat as siblings do. Ginger charged across the street. She had never wandered across before, but she dashed in between them, and the fight was dispelled. It was comforting to know that she would do the same for our sons.

We were fortunate to have her company for almost 12 years. During that time, we developed a ritual that when my husband and I went to bed, she would follow. She slept at the foot of the bed, so she could be close to us.

When the boys grew older, they began to stay up later than my husband and me. Ginger chose to stay downstairs and keep the boys company.

When my husband and I went to bed, we would close the bedroom door. Sometimes, when Ginger wanted in, she would stand outside the door and whimper. She waited very patiently, but if she wasn't let in soon, she would give a soft bark just in case we hadn't heard her whimper. One of us would then get up and let her in. She, immediately, would go to her place at the foot of the bed.

This loving and loyal creature reached the point when she had to be lifted to go outside. The time finally came when we needed to let her go. We had to make the heart wrenching decision. My husband and I faced this together. We said goodbye to Ginger for the last time at the vet's office. All the good times had past much too quickly. No more soccer games, no more punctured soccer balls, and no more bicycle races around the block.

That night we closed the bedroom door. Just as we were drifting off to sleep, we heard a soft bark at the door. Of course, we opened it. Ginger, our loyal Golden, wanted to say goodbye.

Judy M.

Sweety, AKA Gnarly

Sweety was a previously owned Calico Cat. She adopted me when she was expecting a litter. The former owners had named her after an expression used in the movie, "Fast Times at Ridgemont High." Gnarly meant good or "far out." I thought the name didn't suit her, even though she was very good. Most often, I called her Sweety.

When she came to my home, she was about a year old. After she had her kittens, I had her spayed.

We got along just fine. I lived alone and worked five days a week, and I felt we needed each other. She waited each day to greet me in the carport. She was pretty talkative and would answer not only me, but my friends and family as well. Sweety was like a chatty little girl.

Sweety had the run of our home, and she had special places to nap. In the kitchen, near the counter, she had a special chair. When she sat there, she knew she would get a lot of attention.

One day I noticed she was breathing faster than usual. Her stomach was fluttering in and out. My first thought was that she had a hairball. I put a bit of mayonnaise on her paw for her to lick off and to possibly relieve the problem.

Another day passed, and she would not eat. She looked so healthy in every other way that I didn't suspect anything serious could be going on. I took her to the vet to make sure that she was just fine. Some tests were run, and they showed a large amount of malignant fluid in her lung cavity. That explained the fluttering stomach. She was using her diaphragm muscles to let her lungs expand and contract. The test results were a death sentence. I allowed the doctor to put her to sleep.

I couldn't face going in the back to see her in a cage and watching her die. Matters like this are different for everyone, and each must face the situation in their own way.

I was so heartbroken to go home alone and without my beloved companion. I didn't want to face the fact that she was gone from me. I didn't want to believe it.

After several days of despair and much crying, I decided I should be thankful for the time we had together. I thanked God for sending me such a precious gift. My heart was immediately lightened, and I had a feeling of peace.

One night soon after that, I was drifting off to sleep, and she came for a visit. I felt her jump onto the bed and walk awkwardly over my shins as she used to do. This visit only lasted a few seconds. I froze and waited for another sign, but none came.

I was so moved that she had come back. I told my mother about Sweety's visit, and she too felt that it was Sweety. It was then that I began to heal, though slowly.

Her visit, I feel, told me she had forgiven me for leaving her behind at the vet's office.

This incident happened 13 years ago, and it is still so vivid to me. She was my dearest friend. I look forward to seeing her again.

Evelyn

Beau

I was working as a veterinary technician in Houston, at an animal shelter, when Beau was brought in. He was four weeks old and had just begun to eat a bit of soft food. He was tiny, and pale yellow, and much too young to be away from his mother. Little did I know that he would grow into a handsome hunk. My heart went out to him, and I took him home. He needed to be fed about every two to four hours.

We spent a lot of time just playing. He never cared for the usual toys unless they were edible. His favorite game was "retrieve the stick." The bigger the stick, the better the game. He also liked to be near me and sit on my lap, all 70 pounds of him. I would sit on the ground, and he would come over and sit his rear right in my lap.

Beau was my best buddy and soul mate. He was my sole support as we went through difficult times together. Many times we moved cross-country with our belongings in the back of my pick-up truck. He was happy wherever I was. Actually, the feeling was mutual.

Fourteen years later, Beau developed problems that couldn't be relieved by medication. Sadly, the time came for euthanasia. He died in my arms. This was a tragic time for me. I wasn't ready for him to go. I dreamed of him nightly for such a long time.

I hadn't experienced a dream or vision of an animal before, although I have had some unusual experiences. When I was 15 years old, I was hospitalized with bibasilar pneumonia. I had, what I believe, was a near death experience. My relatives were standing around my bed, and the preacher was reading from the bible. I saw this from the upper right hand corner of the room. It, evidently, was not my time to die, and I was able to go home at the end of a week.

When my father died, I hadn't been able to talk to him for almost a year. I agonized over that for such a long time. My feeling of neglect really bothered me. One night my dad came to me. It wasn't a dream. I sat up in bed, and my dad was standing at the foot of the bed, clear as day. Neither of us said anything. He just looked at me then turned around and left. I felt he was telling me that I could go on and that he was OK.

My grandmother's family was Appalachian and there are stories of visions and premonitions. Maybe, it is a familial trait.

One dream, in particular, was very real. In this dream, Beau came to me and sat on my lap. I asked, "God, please give me another dog like Beau." I am a spiritual person but do not consider myself religious, and I can't explain why I said that in my dream. There never would be another dog that could replace Beau.

The next Saturday, I went to the animal shelter and chose the ugliest puppy there and named her Julep. I was afraid no one would choose her, and I knew I could give her a lot of love and attention. She certainly is not Beau, but she does like to sit in my lap, and that, to me, is a connection between the two of them. I believe that, in the dream, Beau was telling me it was OK to bring Julep home.

Roxann Zellers

Sadie

She was my first dog and a Mini-Schnauzer. Sadie flew in from Spokane on a bitter, cold Montana night. She was so tiny amidst the crate full of shredded newspaper, I thought that the breeder forgot to send the dog. Then Sadie shook herself out, stepped out of the crate, and piddled on the airport floor. It was a preview of coming attractions.

I called Sadie my sobriety dog. She came to me at a very difficult time of my life. I had no idea how to have relationships or build a new life. I really believe that Sadie came to teach me. She was like my alter ego. She was loving, kind, gentle, and if that didn't work — bite them on the leg. Every behavior I ever had that needed to go, Sadie had also. Sadie was my external mirror and showed me more about myself than I ever wanted to know.

For behavior changes, I enrolled her in obedience school. Sadie didn't much take to a leash, and the choke chain had to go. She stood stiff legged and wouldn't move. Each time I gently tugged on the leash and said, "Heel," Sadie threw up. We got thrown out of obedience school.

Maybe she needed a sister. We got Rosie.

Sadie went to doggy day care when I was out of the house. The sitter told my husband, Ron, and me that Sadie loved to watch ice-skating. We thought that she was nuts. We later found that she was right. Skating quickly took a back seat, however, once Sadie discovered animals appeared on TV too. She barked at everything that crawled, swam or flew. She could even pick the animals out of cartoons.

Her favorite commercials were the "toilet duck" and the "Little Caesar's" ad that featured a poodle doing the bunny hop. She sat diligently and waited for them to appear. She was especially fond of the "Westminster Dog Show" and the program "Northern Exposure." As soon as the "Northern Exposure" theme music started, she charged to the set, trembled with anticipation, and waited for the moose to stroll across the screen. When it appeared, and it always did, she went ballistic.

As dear as she was to me, she was the epitome of every breeding horror story you've ever read. Her medical problems were endless, and the bills were staggering. It didn't matter. She was my best friend.

At age five, she suffered stroke-like symptoms and almost died. Ron and I took turns sitting, around the clock, with her day after day. Eventually, she improved, trouper that she was, but Sadie lost the vision in her left eye and some of the use of her left limbs. No longer able to go on long walks with us, but howling if left behind, a baby backpack was the perfect solution. She loved it.

Sadie accompanied me through the best and worst years of my life; getting sober, changing jobs, the deaths of two grandparents, getting married (she came to our very formal wedding reception), moving, and the toughest chapter of all, losing my brother, Larry, to AIDS. Six months after Larry died in my arms, Sadie also slipped away at the age of eight. When she died, I didn't think that I could bear it.

The night after Sadie died, I was begging for a sign that I'd made the right decision and that it was really her time to go. I was still torn. I stared out at the cold, dark sky hoping Sadie was warm and happy somewhere. She had always hated the cold.

Suddenly, beautiful green lights danced across the sky. I thought that I was losing it. I called Ron to the window, and I was relieved when he gasped, "Wow, it's the Northern Lights!" No moose, no theme song, but perfectly reminiscent of Sadie. I went to sleep holding the little green sweater that she loved close to me.

When I awakened the next morning, the prayer plant in our bedroom had bloomed for the first time. It bloomed again, a second time, on the first anniversary of her death. It was a meaningful sign for me. When it didn't bloom the next anniversary, I was devastated. Then it bloomed on Ron's birthday instead, on March seventh. Since that time, I've come to know that it always blooms on a significant day.

One night during that first week, I woke up feeling Sadie's body next to me in bed. It only happened once. Another night I was just missing her so much and looked up, and this enormous falling star went by. It was so bright, at first I thought a plane was going down. It looked like it would fall through my window. I've since come to associate falling stars with Sadie also.

Sadie had a very annoying habit of walking across the TV or VCR remote controls. This usually happened just at the climax of the show. The day after she died, I was watching the news when the TV suddenly clicked off. I automatically yelled, "Sadie, stop it!" forgetting that she was no longer with me. It happened every day for a week. I told Ron, but he didn't believe me. Then — it happened to him. Maybe she hung around a little longer, until I was ready to say goodbye too.

After Sadie's death, I wanted to honor her memory. After much thought, Ron and I were thinking about getting involved with animal shelters. We are extremely busy people, but we felt the need to work with animals. That weekend the prayer plant bloomed again. It was a positive sign for us. We now manage Web sites, for 21 of 22 Montana shelters, providing daily maintenance. The main Web site is Montana Pets on the Net, at www.montanapets.org. We're very active in shelters and rescue. I feel that we did her memory proud.

Dianne Armstrong

Author of *Home Again, Home Again, Jiggety Jig.* Her e-mail address is dogs4@juno.com.

Siam

Siam was adopted from an animal shelter in Wisconsin and showed signs of abuse. Siam was very underweight and sick, and from the looks of her, no one would choose her. We fell in love with each other at first sight. It appeared that her former owner had bred her much too young, and as health problems arose, Siam was sent to the shelter. No kittens came with her, even though she was a nursing mother. I believe her abuse was the cause of the pancreatitis she developed early in her life. It was necessary to put her on a strict diet.

Some time later, I learned she was a Ragdoll. This is a hybrid breed that originated around 1965. Ragdolls started with a cross of a white Persian female and a seal point male Birman. When their offspring were bred with a sable Burmese, the Ragdoll was the result. When they are held in the arms, they tend to go limp; hence, the name Ragdoll.

After a couple of months in our home, which included numerous trips to the vet, Siam gained weight. Her coat filled in, and she was beautiful.

We developed an extremely close relationship, and I felt lucky to have her in my life. Siam was very sweet and gentle. I thought of her as a "poet-philosopher." I lavished all sorts of attention and love on her, as I knew she had been mistreated, and I wanted her to know there was good in the world.

We had so many good times together. One of her favorite games was "get the gopher." I would run my hand under the bedcovers, simulating a gopher run, and she would pounce on my hand in an attempt to kill the creature.

Baseball was another favorite game. I would toss balled up pieces of paper, and she would bat them back at me with her paw. She was ambidextrous, as neither paw was dominant. Baseball evolved into chasing games. She would chase me for a while, and then she would wait for me to chase her.

Siam developed her own play routine. Often she would wake me up at two in the morning. Once that was accomplished, she would race into the living room with me lagging behind. She would then roll around on the floor, belly up, to be petted.

The good times were destined to last only about one year. At year's end, I took her to the vet for her annual vaccinations. She received four shots that day. Within eight hours, she was vomiting every few hours. I immediately took her back to the vet, and he found that her body temperature had dropped. She would no longer eat or drink. For the next two days, she returned to the vet for hydration. This is done by inserting a needle, under the skin, at the nape of the neck. Fluid is then allowed to drain into the space under the skin. The body then gradually absorbs the fluid. There is no discomfort when this is done. The only drawback is having the animal remain still for several minutes.

We spent what was to be our last night together on the floor covered with a blanket. I knew that she was dying.

Even though she was quite ill, her lungs were clear. The following morning at 6:00 a.m., we were back again at the vet's office. She was placed in an oxygen tent, received massive antibiotics, but it was too late. Now she had severe pneumonia. By noontime she was dead.

My personal theory is that she experienced some kind of toxic reaction to that particular combination of vaccinations. The doctor had never seen this type of reaction before.

I was in extreme grief and filled with guilt because I felt responsible for Siam's death.

Two nights later just before dawn, I felt a soft "thump" on the bed and a gentle kneading right at my feet where Siam always slept. At first I was nervous, but I then felt reassured. I told Siam, while she was on the bed, how much I loved her.

She would visit every few months until my husband and I parted. At this time, I moved to a new home. The day before the divorce was finalized, I woke up around dawn feeling lower than low. I felt a great deal of grief and sadness wondering how I could find the emotional wherewithal to cope.

This time, as before, I felt a soft thump on the bed. At first, I thought it was the two kittens we had adopted after Siam's death, but they have grown to such monstrous proportions that I immediately realized it was Siam. She had found me. Siam stayed at my feet, kneading at the blanket, for about five minutes. I swear that I also felt a very gentle purring sensation as well. I told her, again, how much I loved her and what a joy it was to have her in my life. Then she vanished.

Her visit was wonderful. I am convinced Siam knew I was in tremendous need of comfort, and her nurturance reminded me that love is indeed eternal.

Katherine Underwood

Winston

I have been surrounded by animals all of my life. While growing up, my family had a total of seven dogs and oh so many cats. When I left home to strike out on my own, I longed for a dog. Unlike cats, most rentals don't allow dogs, and I never thought of a pet as "disposable," so I waited until I married and bought a home.

The very next month, after we were in our new home, we found an adorable Golden Retriever. We took him home and named him Winston. He was such a delight that we arranged all of our outings based on where he would be welcomed. We hiked many trails in the San Francisco Bay Area Regional Parks and a number of national parks as well. Winston enjoyed swimming in the ocean and various sloughs. We bought bicycles and took him to the Grizzly Point Wild Bird Preserve. He ran alongside and carried his very own backpack.

We had thought of breeding him one day, and as a result, he was never neutered. I have regrets about this. When Winston was around the age of three, he began to run away if the gate or door was opened.

That is how we lost him. It was a Sunday evening, already dark, when I opened the door to pick some lemons in the back yard. Winston dashed out the door and kept running. He ignored my calls as he had better things in mind. I continued throughout the night to look and call for him, but there was no sign of him. He had never before stayed away so long. I work full time, and I finally had to go to bed

Monday night I had a dream or, perhaps, a vision would be a more appropriate word. I felt a movement against the side of the bed, as though a dog stood up and put his paws on the bed. I opened my eyes; the room was clear and filled with light. I saw Winston sitting next to my bed between our two cats, Cleo and Rex. He was looking at me, but his eyes didn't look quite right, and he didn't move. Both the cats looked at me with their normal cat eyes and had their heads slightly tilted.

It was at this time that I awoke, but the room was too dark to see anything clearly. I had a deep ache, like a hole, in the center of my chest. I bent over with both hands on my breast trying to stop the ache and prevent something from escaping.

Later in the day, the vet called and told me that Caltrans had contacted him. Winston had gotten on the Carquinez Bridge and had been hit and killed. The entrance had not been too far from our home, and I suspect that he was coming home.

Four days later, I had another dream. Again, there was movement on the side of the bed. I opened my eyes and saw Winston looking at me with a happy expression. I got up to play with him and told him how glad I was to see him. He rolled around on the floor to get his stomach scratched. His fur was silky, as always, and there was his light musky smell that I remembered so well.

Then he was gone. The room was dark as before, but the heavy ache that I had before was absent. I felt comforted, and I'm sure that was Winston's intention.

A. D. A.

Vincent

I acquired Vincent and his sister, Molly, and they proved to be excellent pets. I formed the strongest attachment to Vinny. Early mornings, he would sit on the windowsill, and together we would watch the sunrise. Then off I would go to work. Vinny waited there on his perch to see me off. He was a handsome orange tiger-stripe cat but was going through a very difficult time with cancer.

He had rallied before, and I hoped he could continue. When he was well enough, I went back to work. Each morning, Vinny got to his window shelf. I told him that it was a good idea. When the sun came up, we could both look out our windows and see the sunrise at the same time; even though, we were not together.

As his illness progressed, he grew much weaker, and at times it was necessary for him to be carried to the litter box. One Saturday I allowed him to eat shrimp, his favorite food, all day. He would do anything to get shrimp, and that was the last meal he ate.

That afternoon, I went up to take a shower. Vinny made his way upstairs, and I found him trying to get on top of the toilet seat, but he was too weak to jump there. It was a place where he had never before shown an interest. He returned there again that evening and the next day. I carried him downstairs and placed him in his chair. He remained there, unless I carried him to the litter box.

Things got very bad about 2:00 a.m. Sunday night into Monday morning. I did everything possible to calm him. Concern got the better of me, and I called my neighbor. We discussed taking him to emergency. He was not having trouble breathing, and I decided to wait a while longer. I couldn't face the possibility of him leaving too soon. I began to read the Rainbow Bridge poem to him over and over. It seemed to calm him. I told him, again, how much I loved him and his sister, Molly. I told him, no matter where he went, he would always have our love with him. After he was rested, he would find a new body and come back to us.

Just before sunrise on Tuesday morning, I carried him to the window, so we could share our last sunrise together. It was the only day out of a week that it didn't rain. I talked to Vinny and told him how sad I was that I had been unable to hold Toby, my other cat, who had gone on to Rainbow Bridge. I held Vinny his last seventy two hours. Neither one of us slept for three days. I talked to him constantly. If I stopped he would cry.

I called the vet, and he came at 10:00 a.m., and Vinny was gone by 10:15. The vet said it was the most peaceful passing he had ever seen. As we sat in his chair, Vinny was cradled in my arms where he belonged.

On Friday, I made what might have been a mistake. I went to the Humane Society and on impulse took home a cat. She was eight years old and had been in four previous homes. She purrs constantly just like Vinny. For some unknown reason, I had decided I would take her back to the Humane Society. The next morning she walked into the bathroom behind me and jumped up on the toilet as Vinny had been trying to do. She then looked me right in the eye. I wondered if that was a signal Vinny had left her. I knew that she had to stay.

She was gray with green eyes when I got her. Much to my amazement, I find she is now about one-half orange, similar to Vinny, and is taking on many of his traits.

She is a sweet, well-mannered cat, and I could find no reason why she was returned for another placement. At times I feel that she was placed in the other four homes while she waited for me.

Two weeks before Vinny died, I took several pictures of him. When the pictures were developed, there was a streak of pink light coming straight from his head. I feel that it was an aura. That particular photo was in the middle of the roll. No candles or lights were on in the room, and there was no glare from the outside. All the other pictures were fine and showed no distortions.

Without Vinny there is an empty feeling in the house. His spirit is here though. I can feel it. Molly, his sister, feels it also. She stays on their bed, stares into the air, and carries on a conversation with him. There is a short silence as she listens, and then she replies to him.

I am tuned into my pets' emotions and they to mine. I have had two intense dreams or visions of Vinny. They comfort me. His presence is so strong, I don't think he will ever leave. The fact that he is still here with me is more important to me than the dreams.

Dorothy Ann

Yogie Bierra

Yogie was born in March of 1984. He "crossed over" March 23, 1998, two weeks shy of his 14th birthday. He was white with cream or tan markings and was a mix of German Shepherd, Husky, and Labrador Retriever.

He was the first dog that was truly mine, all my responsibility. His food, training, affection, and socialization were all up to me. He was cute, smart, loving, and so playful. Everything he did was just so cute! It was like, "Here I am, love me." As a puppy, he went everywhere with me. As Yogie got bigger, people weren't always so thrilled to have him in their houses, but he continued to go with me to my parents, for rides to the store, and on other short errands.

He could always make me smile and feel good because he loved me no matter what. He was happy to see me when I came home and would "roo," not bark, as soon as he saw me coming. It was his way of talking.

He liked to sleep with me, but in the winter I use an electric blanket, so he would then lie on my pillow.

We went for long walks together, played ball, and did all the fun things we both enjoyed.

Yogi developed a liking for people food, especially meat. He managed to beg cookies, cheese, eggs with toast (of course), chips and dip, strawberry ice cream, and any kind of pizza. He also ate a balanced diet of dog food.

We went through a lot together; a failed marriage, moving to my family's home, another marriage, and another home. At some point in our lives together, he ceased to be a dog and became a dear companion.

When Yogi was six months old, we got a companion for him, another dog, Buffy, who was Lab and Golden Retriever. They became fast friends. We eventually added a Lab to our family, and even though Yogi got older, he continued to play.

I refused to see age creeping up on him. The vet called him geriatric. Soon, way too soon, his eyes became cloudy. Yogi slept a bit more, and his legs began to stiffen, but when I looked at him, all I saw was just my Yogi. When he could no longer get up on my bed, I set up a mound of pillows next to the bed for him. He could still sleep beside me.

Now he began to fall more often. It became necessary to let him outside alone, so the other dogs wouldn't accidentally knock him down. When they were there, it was obvious, he was afraid of falling. The outside steps were a problem as was the slippery kitchen floor, snow, and ice. I decided that boots for him would help, but he hated them and dreaded putting them on to go outside.

The vet suggested a medication that would help his arthritis. The day before his appointment, I discovered a mass on his rear leg. I didn't want to face the fact that the problem was serious. After two biopsies and a x-ray, the diagnosis of cancer was made. To remove the mass would have meant removing the leg. At the age of 13-plus, he probably would not have survived the surgery or recovery. I had never felt so helpless. Five months later the painful decision was made for him to be euthanized.

At times I didn't know if I wanted to live on without him. Yogi was special to me. The other animals didn't help me at this time. My grief lasted a long time.

A short time after Yogi's passing, he came to me in a vision or dream. I saw him standing on all of his four legs. There was no sign of weakness. He was wagging his tail and looked very pristine as though he had been immaculately groomed. There were other dogs with him, but I recognized none of them. He appeared happy when he looked directly at me. Yogi was there for a few seconds, and then he was gone.

One other time, while I was sleeping, I did not dream of him, but I felt him there in the room. It was very powerful and difficult to describe. The next morning I felt very peaceful. Yogi's visit was so profound that I knew it had meaning. His passing has led me on a spiritual search of my own. I am eager to learn and be enlightened.

Many people won't understand the events that often take place after the death of a dear pet. It makes me think of my favorite quote, by Angela Monet, "Those who danced were thought to be quite insane by those who could not hear the music."

Sandy W.

Templeton

Templeton, a rat, was my littlest darling. He died after 18 months of being one of the most lovable and brightest animal companions I had ever owned.

He was a dear little creature. His body was a handsome gray with a white tummy. When I purchased him, he was two months old. Armed with a book on the care of rats and a roomy cage, we set off for home. When I placed him into his new cage, he let out a scream that was so chilling that I hear it to this day.

It took four days before he adjusted to being away from his mom and littermates. During this time, he refused all food. I finally won him over with an ear of yellow corn, which remained his favorite for life. White corn was ignored.

Templeton died of an enlarged spleen. I was devastated and missed him so. He gave me much pleasure and many smiles.

Two days after his passing, I caught a glimpse of him scurrying around all of his favorite hiding places in the house. I continue to see him occasionally. Even though Templeton was a tiny creature, his spirit was enormous.

At times I wonder if our pets have as difficult a time letting go of us as we do of them. It seems that all of my fur-babies have survived physical death. Perhaps I am more receptive to the signs of their presence.

I have found it a good idea for me to get another pet soon after the death of one of my own. I grieve less and have their valuable companionship longer than if I had waited to fully recover from my grief. I have also opened my home and my heart to a pet that needs me.

Chris

Megan

I adopted Megan, a Terrier and Shepherd mix, when she was five weeks old. She was a tri-colored ball of brown, black, and white fur with incredibly blue eyes. All my family has brown eyes, and her eyes fascinated me. She was a true family member from the moment of her adoption. Her transition into our lives went smoothly. During her puppyhood she preferred to sleep on my chest. I think the sound of my heartbeat made her feel more secure.

We spent much of our free time playing games or just sitting quietly. She liked to tug on a toy or her favorite bone. Occasionally she would put her head in my lap to be stroked. We were content just spending time together.

Christmas and family birthdays were especially happy times. Megan was always there to sing Happy Birthday or her favorite Christmas tune, Rudolf the Red-nosed Reindeer. She was quite talented, in the singing department, and seldom missed a beat. We often sang together for no special reason. She would follow me around, while I did household chores, as we sang. Megan seemed to sing just for the joy of it.

All our good times were put on hold, however, when she was diagnosed with lymph node cancer. She had just turned six years old. It was such a trying time. The frustration, of not being able to help her, was devastating. I hated to let her go away from me, and I discussed her situation with the doctor. There was nothing more that could be done for her, and I had to make the painful decision to allow her to go. I was able to hold her and tell her how much I loved her and how much joy she had given me. I returned home and have never been the same since she went away.

About two months after Megan's death, I walked into my son's room, and there were paw prints on the bed. The prints always appeared in the same place where Meg used to lie. All my grief welled up. I missed her so. After I was able to give it some thought, I was consoled that she had come back. The prints continued to appear for a while and then stopped.

Meg has been gone for a little over two years, and I still can hear the thumping sound that she makes as she jumps on my son's bed. Often, when I am in the kitchen preparing dinner, I glance into the dining room, and I see her watching me. I can feel her presence in the house. We had such a close bond; I feel that she will always be near me and in my heart as well.

Paula

Hanzel

We were much too busy to have pets. I work as a court reporter and my husband as an accountant. Our working hours were much too long to devote time to a pet.

One evening, while driving through a forest preserve to reach our home, we saw eyes shining near the roadside. When we stopped to investigate, we saw there were two kittens hidden in the bushes.

The kittens were gathered up and taken home. After they were fed and their needs attended to, we took them to the police station that offers this service in our area, so their owners would be able to claim them.

A few days went by, and they were still homeless. It was evident, they had been abandoned. At this point we felt they were meant to be ours. The brother and sister from the forest were named Hanzel and Gretel.

Hanzel was always a klutz, and I wondered if it would be safe for him to be allowed outside. His supervised visits outside proved to be questionable. He tried to play with some bees and was stung all over his face. On another outside excursion, he injured his leg, which required a visit to the all-night veterinary clinic.

Hanzel enjoyed playing with plastic bags. On one occasion, his head got stuck in the handles, and he raced through the house while the bag chased him. He needed protection from himself, and this quality is what endeared him to me.

We developed a close bond. If I sat, he was on my lap. If I stood, he jumped up on my shoulders. Hanzel enjoyed the ride as I did chores around the house. He seemed to know what I planned to do next. Perhaps it was my body language that may have announced it, but at times I felt it was intuition. Of the many cats that I have had, he is the only one that gave me head butts. That was his way of marking me as friendly territory.

When Hanzel and Gretel were four years old, I bought a Maine Coon kitten, named Kahjee. Gretel resented Kahjee, but Hanzel took on the role of peacemaker. He would lick Kahjee's head and then do the same for Gretel. After a short time, they were comfortable with each other.

Last spring, Hanzel, my beautiful orange and white Tabby, developed hypertrophic cardiomyopathy, a heart condition. His labored breathing was helped by medication, and several pills a day were put in a capsule. This made it a bit easier, as he disliked it so. It was a struggle at every dose.

In September my husband and I went on vacation. Arrangements were made, for a woman from the clinic, to care for the animals and administer the medication.

On the day I returned, she told me that Hanzel had struggled more than usual at his morning dose. His condition did seem to be weaker. That night his breathing was very labored. When morning came, we went to the clinic for him to be examined. His lungs were very congested, and the decision was made to help him go peacefully. I was able to comfort him for the last time.

My husband prepared a eulogy for him. One of his remarks was that Hanzel was the only pet he knew that was mourned by friends as far away as Japan.

In the days that followed, I began to find gelatin capsules in the middle of the floor and in various places in the house. I knew the caretaker would have made sure that Hanzel had swallowed the capsules. How had they escaped regular house-cleanings? I wondered what this could mean. Was it a sign Hanzel was giving me that he was still with me? If Hanzel had spit out the medication, his condition would have deteriorated much sooner. I couldn't come up with a logical answer.

One night, shortly after Hanzel died, I was lying in bed and heard a noise. I hoped it was Hanzel and that he would give me a sign that he was OK. For some reason I became frightened. I longed to feel him bump against me or lie on my pillow, but of course, it didn't happen. Maybe it was my fear that kept him away, even though I longed to have him near.

Several months passed, and I convinced my husband we needed another kitten. Tori was found, and he joined our family. He does many things that Hanzel used to do. Tori also played the role of peacemaker. Hanzel used to sit on top of the warm monitor as I worked on my computer in our home office. Once when I was working on a different computer, Tori sat on the same monitor as Hanzel had, even though it was cold.

On Tori's first visit to the vet, he immediately jumped up on my shoulders as Hanzel used to do. My thoughts had been of Hanzel's last visit there. I feel Hanzel sends me messages through Tori. He has taken on so many of Hanzel's actions, I feel I have been given another chance to share some of our experiences all over again. For that I am grateful.

Alex

54

Chelsea

My son, "Tom," found a small caramel-colored puppy wandering in the streets near his school and brought her home. I made every effort to find her owners to no avail. We quickly became attached to her and decided to keep her and named her Chelsea. She adapted well to our cats and us, and they all slept together on my bed or Tom's. The cats and Chelsea were about the same size and made a handsome trio.

For the first two years, she chewed on everything. We baby-proofed the house to remove anything that might be harmful to her.

Tom and Chelsea developed a very close bond. He taught her to dance on her hind legs and to roll over. Though small, her energy level was a good match for that of her new friend.

A favorite game was "catch me." Chelsea would grab a piece of mail or homework and race through the house with Tom lagging behind. To amuse me, Tom would yell, "She stole my hundred dollar bill!" or, "That is my irreplaceable masterpiece!"

Candy was another item that she sneaked. She hid the telltale wrappers under her bed. When some item was missing, I checked her cache under the bed. Usually it was found there. Once her claw marks were found across the top of a box of Godiva chocolates as though she had tried to pry it open. Fortunately, she didn't eat any, as even a small amount could have made her ill. Chelsea also had a liking for cake. One day I made a banana cake for Tom to take to school. I placed it in a bag and set it on the floor near the door to make sure he wouldn't forget it. When it was time for Tom to leave, the bag had disappeared. We finally found the empty paper bag in a corner. She devoured the whole thing and binged at any opportunity.

Because of Tom, who would send for some cereal box trinket using Chelsea's name, she was on tele-marketer and junk mail lists. She was entered in contests, and she still receives mail in her name. I don't mind that type of mail. It is a fond reminder of our Chelsea.

This dear little pet graced the family with her presence for 17 years. As she grew older, her vision was severely impaired, and her joints became very painful. When she reached the point where she couldn't get out of her bed, I knew that it was finally time to ease her suffering.

I made the necessary preparations and followed through with the heaviest of hearts. I cried until my eyes were so swollen that I could barely see. I just went to bed and longed for her to be back again.

That evening, Chelsea visited me in a dream or vision. White clouds were around an elevation on which sat a little caramel-colored dog, who looked like Chelsea. As I put my arms around this little dog, I felt her warmth and smelled her sweet fur, which always reminded me of a mink coat, and all my senses were intensified. This was more real than reality. My first thought was it couldn't be her as she was no longer with us, yet I knew that it was Chelsea. I cherished the time I had with her in this vision. I immediately thought of Michelangelo's painting of Creation. The vision was that glorious, and I felt comforted.

Next morning, much of the pain was gone, and I felt elation and acceptance. There was some sorrow, but I was grateful that I had been able to hold her one last time.

My heaven won't be complete without each and every one of my beloved pets.

Mimi

Demitasse

Demi, as we called her, was teacup size and even in adulthood never weighed more than four pounds. She was a mixture of Maltese and French Poodle. This combination proved to be an excellent balance and produced a smart and loving family member. Her hair was long, white, and silky. As a puppy, she was a ball of fluff.

My husband would tease me and say Demi looked more like a cat than a dog because she was the size of a young kitten. It didn't help that when she was wet from her bath, she looked like a shivering and drowned rat.

Because of her size, she went with me on shopping trips. She could easily fit in my handbag, but I usually carried her in one arm. Once a clerk at the register tried to pluck her from my arm to check her price tag and ring her up. I pulled back, and the clerk was astounded when the "toy" moved.

Demi was like a perpetual two-year-old who needed watching all the time. There were times when her antics were trying, but I now believe she was just very curious about everything around her. She was much too intelligent to lie around and do the usual doggy things. She preferred to interact with people, but when left alone, she provided her own entertainment.

One day when home alone, she figured out how to open a box of chocolates that was left on the coffee table. Demi had sampled all of them leaving little teeth marks in each one. Evidently, they weren't to her liking, but she tasted each of them just in case. Had she eaten some, it could have proven fatal. When we came home, her adorable white face was covered with the evidence. Still, her expression was one of innocence, and she used those wiles to escape being scolded.

One night her adventurous spirit led her to investigate the fireplace. The next morning we awakened to find an excited, black and gray puppy sitting on an equally black and gray carpet! Fortunately, the charcoal she had eaten was not a health hazard.

She learned to open a cupboard door where the garbage bag was located. She ate a few chicken bones. They are an absolute no-no for animals because they splinter. She had to be taken to the vet and was treated for internal bleeding. It was necessary to give her oil a couple of times a day. I put the oil over her food, but she wouldn't eat it very well. I tried it over bread with the same result. I was concerned she wasn't getting enough. One day I reached for the bottle of oil, and Demi sat up and begged. I offered it to her from the spoon, and she eagerly lapped it off. Evidently, she liked it neat or straight.

One windy day, she stood too close to the screen door, and it blew open and then closed on her leg. Another trip to the vet for a splint solved that problem. She used her broken leg to advantage. Moving around was no problem, but at times she would limp a bit to get extra attention. I pretended to go along with it and told her she was a brave little soldier.

I had a part time job at that time, and Demi was left alone a few hours a day. A neighbor informed me that Demi barked the whole time I was away. She suggested we get Demi a pet to keep her company. We finally found a black Poodle, named Yvette of Fountain Blue, who was being abused by the family she was with. When I picked up a broom or something similar, she would cower and cringe. It took some time for us to win her trust, but she did respond. The two dogs got along very well. Demi now had a companion. When we were away or at work, there were two dogs that barked. I checked back with the former owners and was told that Yvette seldom barked. Demi taught her well.

As Yvette aged, she lost her sight, and Demi volunteered to be her eyes. Yvette's shoulder would hug Demi's hindquarters. They ran through the house as before, and Demi would even take Yvette outside when it was necessary. It was a very touching sight to watch them. Tiny little Demi was a nanny to her charge, and it was evident that she enjoyed her job.

From the age of six weeks to the time of her leaving, at 10 years of age, the time passed much too quickly.

She suffered a heart attack very late one evening. My macho husband and I sat on the bed and cried the rest of the night. For all his teasing that she was a foo-foo excuse for a dog, she had certainly won his heart as well.

I have had pets in my life for so many years, but Demi was my "special" one. She had a favorite tree in the backyard, and that is where we buried her.

I felt her spirit around me for a very long time. At night I could hear her bark, and I would jump out of bed to let her in at the patio door. I was not fully awake and wondered how I could have been so irresponsible to have left her outside before going to bed. When I opened the door, I was again faced with the fact that Demi was no longer with us. This was repeated over and over again. The pain was difficult. Today, 30 years later, my eyes still tear up when I think about her. Her picture remains in my wallet. It is more faded than my memories of her. I will always miss her.

Ruth

Ernie

My husband, Steve, and I met Ernie when we went browsing at a flea market. We were not looking for another dog, but then I saw Ernie. He and his sister were sitting on a display table. He was black and tan in color and his sister, Eleanor, was somewhat bigger and tan. He was such a tiny little thing. He could fit in my hand. Steve had walked on, but I asked the owner if I could show him to my husband. When she agreed, I carried him to show him off.

While walking back to the table, we discussed the fact that we had two dogs already. If we weakened and selected one, it should probably be the female. The trouble was I had already fallen in love, and at that point, no one could have pried Ernie away from me. That is how he came to live with us. We discussed changing his name, but he really did look like an Ernie to us.

The former owner said he was a mixed breed with Poodle being dominant. There was no way he was Poodle. If there was any, it was hidden much too deep to be seen. He looked every bit a Terrier.

Ernie and I were soul mates, and he loved Steve too. Ernie ruled the household. He went everywhere with us. We visited friends, camped, and traveled. He was happiest when he rode on the snowmobile or perched on the front of the quad motorcycle.

He had this funny thing about going in the water. Ernie would wade in until he was knee deep and then all at once flop over on his side. He would then stand up, walk out, and shake himself off. Everyone would be in hysterics as they watched him. This was repeated many times over. Perhaps, it was too warm a day, or it was the ham in him. I suspect it was the latter, and he enjoyed the attention.

We trained him to stay off the furniture. He had a small wicker bed in the living room, where he slept most of the time. One morning when my alarm went off, I went directly to the living room, before getting showered and dressed for work. Much to my surprise, my rocking chair was rocking silently in the dark. I felt the seat cushion, and it was warm. Ernie was in his bed snoring as usual. I turned on the light, approached Ernie, and asked him if he had been on the chair. He slowly raised his head, as if he had just awakened, and looked at me as if to say, "How could you think I would do such a thing?" As an actor, he was an absolute porker. From that point on, he never bothered to hide sleeping on the chair or the sofa.

Ernie was very smart. He was able to pick out any toy that you asked. I never figured out how he did it other than being smart. We tested him many times by calling out toys in any order, and he never failed.

I said earlier that Ernie ruled the household. Even at 16 pounds, he bossed the cats that were larger than him and even the Rottweiler. It was quite a sight to see this little one hanging off the jowl of the 125-pound giant. The Rottweiler would also swing him in circles when they played a game of tug of war. Ernie held on no matter what! It was quite a ride. This was Ernie's own version of Disneyland. He gave us so much pleasure and many fond memories.

We visited Hawaii when Ernie was three years old. We couldn't take him because of the quarantine requirements, so my father stayed with our animals. We came home two weeks later. I rushed in the house to see my Ernie, and he looked at me and walked away. I was heartbroken, and it took four days before he forgave me for leaving him at home. I tempted him with some of his favorite tidbits, which were apples, bananas, watermelon, squash, and cherry tomatoes.

He was healthy, and it was only around his 17th year that he began to experience problems with arthritis. He could no longer jump up on the sofa, so I put one of the cushions on the floor to make a stair for him. Ernie's eyes became cloudy with cataracts, but the vet said that he didn't need surgery. His hearing lessened as well.

When he reached 18, I needed to face the fact that his time with me was limited. Occasionally he would have a spurt of energy, but it was rare. We had a bad winter during his last year, and he developed Bronchitis. It was treated with antibiotics. He developed high blood pressure from coughing. The cold weather aggravated his arthritis.

I agonized over his age and poor health. I didn't want to make the final decision. I was afraid I wouldn't know when it was time. I prayed that he would go in his sleep. Well, neither Ernie nor God cooperated and gave me the answer I wanted.

One day Ernie walked across the kitchen floor and fell. He looked up at me with a look that said, he did not want to live if his body did not cooperate. He wanted to have dignity. I called the vet and made the appointment for three days later. I spent those days loving him and doing the things he enjoyed.

The ride to the vet's office, on June 4, 1999, was the worst ride I have ever taken. I did for him what I have made my family promise to do for me (if I am ever at the place where I do not have quality of life). No matter how much I rationalize, it doesn't ease the pain.

Ernie's ashes, with his collar on top of the box, are on my dresser along with his picture beside it. There are two candles from his ceremony near the box of ashes. He still greets me each morning — just in a different way.

I missed him terribly, and I prayed that he would come and visit me. I wanted to make a connection with him, but nothing was happening. I must have been trying too hard, and I finally gave up. After about six weeks, he came to me. It was night and I awakened to see my Ernie across the room. I called for him to come to me, but he remained where he was. All I wanted to do was hold him one more time. I was quite upset that he didn't respond. He told me with his eyes that everything was fine and that he was OK. He looked healthy, and the arthritis didn't seem to bother him.

I felt this great peace, but I still wanted to hold him. I now realize he was on a spiritual plane. He comforted me in the only way he could. Hopefully, he will visit again someday. If this means I am crazy, then I'll gladly be crazy because Ernie's visit meant the world to me!

I still miss him so, but I feel there will be a part of Ernie in the next dog we get. We are not looking, but I know one will find me just as Ernie did. I think Ernie will see to it.

Ernie
December 1979 – June 4, 1998.

Thank You for Being My Friend.
The gifts you have given me cannot be seen.
    They are in my heart and in my soul.
Your unconditional love
    unmatched by anyone or anything.
The feeling you have given me, which I carry within,
    is more precious than any tangible thing.
We are "Soul Mates" forever.

Laurie Darling

Fritz

I am a political freelance writer/designer. Even though I have a hectic schedule, there are many times when a pet could share my busy days. While driving home from work in June 1989, I decided to stop at the King County Humane Society in Bellevue, Washington.

My previous pet, Baron, had died about 18 months earlier from a heart aneurysm. I knew I needed a dog for a companion, as I have been around dogs all my life.

There was a vast array of dogs at the pound, and the selection of just one was difficult. I wanted all of them. I went from cage to cage, observing them, hoping for something that would help me make a decision.

In one cage were two brothers, four months old, described as "Shepherd Mix." One was black, furry, and bigger than the other, who was blonde and scrawnier. Their names were Bear and Jake. The black puppy immediately came forward when I approached the cage, stuck his nose through the mesh, and licked my hand. I told the attendant that I wanted to take him to the get acquainted area. I had already made up my mind that his name would be Fritz. I could immediately see he was intelligent, obedient, and affectionate. He even knew how to "fetch," and he sat when I told him to do so; he would stay in place on command and wait there until he was called. His eyes, big as chocolates, convinced me that he was the dog I wanted to go home with me.

I brought him home to our one acre of land on the Sammamish Plateau, northeast of Issaquah, Washington. He weighed 38 pounds, which was quite an armful for me.

He was a rather strange looking puppy, and my husband, Vern, and I could not decide exactly what he was. We consulted with the vet on Fritz's first visit. We were told that he was probably a mixture of Golden Retriever, Black Labrador, and German Shepherd. This proved to be a glorious combination. When he was mature, he looked like a big, black Golden Retriever. There were golden highlights in his coat, a white marking on his chest, webbed toes like a Lab, but a long nose like a Shepherd. He was so handsome and got numerous compliments and admiring glances when we were out together.

When Fritz was a puppy, we had a deluge of baby toads in the Beaver Lake area, where we live. Thousands of the tiny amphibians were all over the place! Fritz decided they looked like something to eat. He ate so many of them, I finally had to scold him and tell him ... if he kept doing that, his eyes would turn slitty and yellow, his skin all warty, and he'd go ree-beep instead of woof ... and hop rather than run. He just looked at me, yawned, then brushed a few toads out of his way with a paw.

Tennis balls fascinated Fritz. He brought home dozens of them. Lord only knows where he found them, but sometimes he'd appear at the end of the day with three or four of them crammed into his mouth. He also brought me some baseballs, a mitt, and a cat collar. I still have no idea where they came from.

He was truly a character and had a personality all his own. He loved most anything we ate, so I had to be careful to keep human food away from him. He adored tuna fish sandwiches and several times gobbled up Vern's sandwiches when he left the room momentarily. He ate radishes, cantaloupe, onions, green salad, pizza, tomatoes, green beans, carrots, peas, rice ... you name it. He was not a picky eater, and we constantly had him on a diet. He weighed 115 pounds at one time, and I told people I didn't want a puppy who weighed more than me! I didn't want to give him much human food, but I bought dog food that had vegetables, meat, and rice in it.

He loved to ride in the car with his head hanging out the rear window, ears flying in the wind, and tongue flapping. He accompanied me when I conducted the 1990 Census for part of the Sammamish Plateau. I felt very safe. If anyone gave me any guff, Fritz would stick his head out the rear window, growl, and bare his two-inch fangs. I found that people were more cooperative when Fritz was with me.

He was a wonderful watchdog ... so wonderful that he went through a windowpane when an UPS man, who he thought looked suspicious, came to deliver a package. No damage was done to either the petrified UPS man ... or Fritz. After that episode, I called him Super Dog — able to leap through windows in a single bound and not a scratch on him.

When he was younger, he liked to crawl under my bed and lie there, particularly if there was a thunderstorm. One day when he was about seven months old, I heard a horrible ky-yii-ing coming from the back of the house. I raced to the bedroom and found my Fritz stuck under the bed. I had to lift the bed up, so he could free himself. He never tried that again, but whenever there was thunder (which is rare in the Northwest) he'd come running to wherever I was in the house and try to hide behind me or under something. Fireworks, gunshots, and other loud noises didn't faze him.

Just past his ninth birthday, my gentle creature developed an incurable cancer, and it was necessary to eliminate his pain by euthanasia. I was inconsolable. About ten days after his death, before going to sleep, I prayed that I would receive some sign that Fritz was content and safe. I had just dozed off to sleep when I sensed a presence. It felt as though something was brushing against the bed. I opened my eyes to see Fritz standing next to my bed looking at me as he had so often done when he wanted to awaken me. The light from the television allowed me to see him clearly. I could feel his breath on my bare arm. At first, I was totally freaked, but I realized this was what I had asked for. Fritz then turned around, and still brushing against the bed, walked to the foot, and stood in profile. I saw him so clearly. He then looked over his shoulder as if to ask me something. I told him it was fine if he wanted to sleep at the foot of the bed, and he could do so anytime he wished. Fritz shook, and I could hear the tags rattle on his collar before he lay down.

I am convinced that Fritz's spirit came to let me know that he will always be with me in spirit ... if not in body. I went to sleep feeling a bit of healing had taken place in my heart.

Anne Witte

Bella

Bella was conceived around Mother's Day, 1984, when I was present, and I helped deliver her when she was born on July 7. Bella was the only girl in a litter of six Brittany Spaniels. She was very easy to train because she simply copied what her mother, Fanny, did.

She had no interest in toys and preferred being with people who were special friends. She had only one true dog friend, Chloe, and about half a dozen favorite humans whom she trusted completely. Most special to her were Uncle Bob and Auntie Terry. She was wary of children but tolerated them. She was never aggressive but would stand her ground and defend herself when appropriate.

She was not fond of trips in the car unless assured that she was going "bye-bye for a run." If we took any route other than the one she knew, she assumed she was going to the vet's office. More often than not, she was right!

Running the levees and exploring the irrigation ditches around Discovery Bay, California, was what she lived for — especially if it involved chasing ducks and jackrabbits! Well into her 13th year, she was still "hunting" for pheasant and would point motionlessly until the pheasant burst out of the undergrowth.

Although she preferred quiet rides in our small El Toro sailboat on Indian Slough, she did cautiously enjoy speedboat rides. She would stand in the bow of the boat and let her ears and tongue flap in the wind. Usually, we would head to Suicide Beach, on a small island in Old River, for a picnic. She could swim and run along the shore without restraint. We had such great times together.

In the springtime, when the hills along Vasco Road were green and blooming with mustard, we took many hikes around the countryside. More than anything else during those hikes, she loved to roll and squirm in nice fresh cow dung. She didn't seem to mind the fragrance, but she was definitely not nice to be near.

My training as a physical therapist came in handy when Bella became a sick, geriatric dog. We struggled with her illness for about two-and-a-half months. Her favorite food was cat food, when she could sneak some. When she became ill and showed no interest in eating, I tried to entice her with cat food. When this failed, we knew the situation was grim.

As heartbreaking as it was, I would not have missed the start of her final journey for anything. I held her as she took her last breath and settled into my arms on July 1, 1998. Just six days shy of her 14th birthday, our dear Bella was peacefully euthanized at home. She lay in a favorite napping spot under a colorful beach umbrella surrounded by her favorite people and kitty sisters. Several birds could be heard in the background.

When Bella died, for the first time in 19 years, we had no dog to greet us at the door after work or when returning from a trip. Ironically, we left on a vacation trip on the day of her passing. I would have canceled it in a heartbeat had there been any hope of saving her.

When we returned the following week, I slept fitfully the first night. I awakened during the night and distinctly heard the familiar click – click – click of her toenails on the kitchen floor as she headed toward the bedroom. I feel that her spirit was looking for me and wondering where I had been for the past week. More than once I have heard the metal tags on her collar jingling just as they did whenever she would shake out her coat. The first time it happened, I hurried out onto the rear porch expecting to see her on her favorite patch of lawn.

Now, after a long period of mourning, I feel that I am ready for another dog. It is a credit to Bella that I can accept another dog into my life and my heart.

I have not heard her footsteps since that night. I feel she was satisfied knowing I was home. Bella was a miracle, a joy, and a blessing, and God, I miss her! I haven't seen her yet, but I'll never stop looking.

Joann

Cocoa

Cocoa was a gorgeous creature. His hair was long and black, and he had large green eyes - like a cat you might see on a Halloween card. He knew he was handsome and would sit and pose wherever he stopped, except when I had my camera at the ready.

He wasn't terribly brave and would hide each time the doorbell rang and when visitors came. He weighed about 12 pounds, but he could out-wrestle my other cat, Jax, who was much larger. Cocoa could pin him on his back in seconds.

Both were inside cats, but Jax liked to take walks with me while on a leash. Cocoa was too frightened to go out and would cry until Jax returned from his outing. Though he acted timid at times, he had a real attitude. He called the shots in the household.

Cocoa's favorite game was playing with a crumpled ball of paper. He could bat one around for hours. If there wasn't one in sight, he would dump the contents of a wastebasket and find one that was suitable. If that failed to yield one to his liking, he would go into the bathroom and take a dried flower from a bowl of potpourri. As you saw from his photo, it was also a favorite place to hang out in the wash basin.

As mischievous as he was, he seemed to respond very well to commands of "down," "come here," "out," and (of course) "no," and "who wants a cookie?"

At bedtime he would jump up at the foot of the bed and gingerly walk up to my pillow, his hair just barely brushing against me, to let me know that he was there.   Each evening, he checked out the window near the bed before he rested his head on my pillow and went to sleep.

He was my best friend for three years.   Not long before he died, I remember saying to myself one day, "Look at me.   My closest and best friend is a cat."

I had just found a photographer who took pet pictures, but before I could book a sitting, my Cocoa died.   He would have looked so handsome.

Cocoa came to visit me several weeks after his death.   I had just gotten into bed, and into my usual comfortable position, when I felt his fur and smelled his fragrance.   I felt him jump up on the foot of the bed, make his way to the window, and then settle-in on my pillow. I had forgotten, momentarily, he was no longer with me.   When I realized this, I felt that he had come to say good-bye.   I was grateful he made that visit.   It gave me another opportunity to just be near him again as I was not there to comfort him when he needed me.

Cocoa died from kidney failure, and for a while, was unable to control his bladder.   When I had to go out, I would confine him to his carrier in my room.   One day when I returned home from my son's ballgame, I found his carrier empty and a strong odor of urine in my room.   He had died there, and my older son found him and buried him, before I returned home.

I was stricken with grief and phoned my best friend that evening. She advised me to open the window and free his spirit to the outside world, so he would be able to rest.   She explained that this was an old Italian custom.   It was in the heat of summer, and the house was tightly shut with the air conditioner on.   I didn't believe her and resisted the idea for some time.   Finally, she just asked me to do it for her.   I sat up in bed, in the dark, and opened the window.   A chilly fog appeared, passed by my legs toward the window, and disappeared taking the odor with it.   My Cocoa's spirit was free.

Though stricken with grief, Cocoa's appearance lessened it somewhat. It is so difficult to let one's best friend go without you. I hope that he will come again for another visit. His spirit will always be welcome.

Denise Chalow

Hobo

In 1984, I worked as a bookkeeper at a nursing home in Florida. I met Hobo only because a social worker would bring animals each week to visit with the patients. An animal shelter was nearby, and it proved to be advantageous to both the shelter and the patients. It was a great opportunity to socialize the animals and for the patients to interact with them.

On one occasion the social worker brought in two puppies. She was quite taken with one puppy and wanted to take him home to show her husband. The shelter required that both of them be taken home and brought back the following day. I volunteered to take the other one home and promptly fell in love.

Early the next morning, I went to the shelter and adopted him. From then on, he was my Hobo. He was a German Shepherd mix with typical markings and floppy ears.

I was in a very turbulent relationship at that time. My partner and I were constantly breaking up and moving in or out. Hobo was a constant in my life. He accepted and loved me for myself.

Each morning, I got up an hour early so we could spend time playing ball and just have fun. Hobo especially enjoyed riding in the car. Usually, he had his head out the window or was staring over my shoulder with his front feet on the back of the driver's seat. Another special treat was swimming in lakes, pools or the ocean. Hobo was a great water dog. He was fearless.

I spoiled him rotten. By that, I mean he received attention from me most all of my spare time. I always made him a special treat each week. Most often, it was boiled chicken and rice. The other times, I boiled soup bones in beef or chicken broth with rice.

His sweet disposition endeared him to everyone he met. Hobo went to work with me once a week to assist in patient therapy. When he approached patients, he sat in front of them, offered his paw, gave them a lick, and then played ball with them. He seemed to be aware that the patients were fragile and was always gentle in his play.

There was a bit of jealousy if he spent more time with one patient than another. Hobo loved the attention and spread his love around.

When he was about 11 years old, he began to exhibit signs of hip dysplasia. I took him to a specialist, and we discussed hip replacement. I felt he was a bit old for it, and I needed time to think it over.

Unfortunately, six months later, a malignant tumor was discovered in his left-rear leg. It was inoperable, and the vet put him on prednisone for the pain. This medication eventually caused a severe case of bloat, and he had to have emergency surgery very late one night. Hobo was such a trouper through it all.

I took him to a homeopathic vet to find something that would help him. He received accupressure to relieve the pain. He did seem to get a bit better, but emotionally he was withdrawing from me. I now wonder if he knew that his time was near.

He began to sleep outside. Hobo was an air conditioner junkie, and yet he wanted to sleep outside in the heat. He had never done this in all of his 11-plus years. He lost his appetite, and I spoon fed him.

The pain worsened, and he had trouble walking. I anguished over what to do. One morning I woke up at 5:00 a.m., and I rushed outside to check on him. He hardly raised his head off the dirt and looked me straight in the eyes, and what I saw was, "Enough Mom, I've had enough."

I called the vet, who had treated him for almost 12 years, and asked him to come over and ease my friend's pain. As quickly as he came into my life, he left.

I began a year of struggle, depression, and guilt. During my worst times, I felt him near me. Many times when I drove to work, I would smell him in the car with me. I felt him there as well. When I didn't feel him near, I felt a great emptiness. A few times when I was sleeping, I felt his leg over my back as he had always done.

On one occasion when I was in the bedroom, I cried and prayed for Hobo to show me a sign. When I left the bedroom, my husband, a non-believer, said that he had seen a white mist in the living room while I prayed.

I often felt badly that my husband saw it and not me. It has been two years now, and I never hear him anymore. I wish I did. I miss him terribly. Although I have two more dogs, they will never replace Hobo or the special bond we had.

Despite what many feel is just a hope of an afterlife, I felt Hobo's essence so strongly; I knew what it meant.

Isabel Souchet

Kitty Man

On a visit to a local mall with my mom, I found my Kitty Man in a pet shop. He was about four or five weeks old. His coloring was unique. He was all white with two black spots at the base of both ears. His tail was black also, as were two smaller spots on his legs. I am not sure of his breed, but he was quite handsome. He was really too young to be away from his mother. There wasn't a love interest in my life at the time, and it was nice that I had more time to devote to him.

In my eyes, he was perfect! He was so adorable. As soon as I walked by his cage, he became very vocal. I had to have him.

My mom told me that I couldn't have him, but I made up my mind that he was going home with me. Mom said he was the ugliest and gangliest thing she had seen. She thought his tail looked as though it belonged on a rat.

We already had Bridgette, a 15-year-old Poodle, at home, and Mom's fear was that it would be too upsetting for her to take a kitten home.

All my arguments won Mom over. I paid the 25 dollars, and we headed home. I told my dad that a boy was in the parking lot, and this was the last kitten. I also said that if he didn't find a home for him, he was going to leave Kitty Man there in the lot.

Dad can be pretty gruff at times, but he is a real softy where animals are concerned. He didn't like the idea of me having a cat, but never asked me to find another home for Kitty Man.

His first week in our home was an upsetting time for me. He was bothered with digestive problems and lost weight. Had he stayed with his mother longer, those problems could have been avoided.

Bridgette played the role of mother. She acted as if she were human, and Kitty Man acted as though he were a dog. They played chasing games. Bridgette chased Kitty Man up the stairs, and he chased her back down. We enjoyed these games too except on Saturday mornings, when we preferred to sleep in.

He proved to be a helpful judge of character for me. Kitty Man would sit in front of visitors, put his front feet on their knees, and stare into their faces. He seemed to enjoy their discomfort.

When I was dating, I watched to see how Kitty Man behaved. If he didn't like my date, he would sit in his intimidating position and at times growl. Usually, he was right on target.

Kitty Man's weight reached 22 pounds as an adult. He never left our yard and was our "guard dog." Our house backed up to a bayou. Occasionally, a Copperhead or Water Moccasin would get under the fence and slither onto the deck. If Kitty Man was inside, he would streak through the house, jump onto the coffee table, and yowl. That way Dad knew it was time for him to encourage the snake to leave.

Bridgette became critically ill, and it was necessary to have her euthanized. Kitty Man was severely affected. He refused to eat, drink or use his litter box for a week. He mourned her passing. I was finally able to coax him out of his depression.

It was about 10 years later when Kitty Man's health failed. He had cystitis a lot when he was younger. Now, at age 15, he was still being troubled with cystitis and arthritis. No options were left to keep him comfortable. A special-diet food could not be tolerated long enough for him to get any nourishment from it. His weight dropped to about six pounds.

I worried and fretted about how I would know when it was time for his last trip to the vet's office. I prayed a lot for guidance. But indeed, I did know when it was time.

Taking him to the vet for the last time was the hardest thing I ever had to do. My vet's office was great. It was a busy Saturday. It's a walk-in sort of place, open 7:00 a.m. to 10:00 p.m., 7 days a week. The counter area was full of people trying to pay and get registered. I stood there with Kitty Man, and my tears started. The girl behind the desk looked up, saw me, and then ushered me into a room. She must have known from my expression what the situation was. I was taken to a room ahead of all the other waiting people.

It was scary not knowing what to expect. The vet set me at ease and told me what would happen. He was very dear and understanding. He allowed me time to talk to my Kitty Man and say good-bye. I assured him that I would stay with him. He was given enough sedation to make him sleep. A final injection was given a short time later, and my sweet fur-baby was gone.

The experience, as it was happening, was serene and calm. As I write this, I feel as though I am reliving it over again. Even though it happened over two years ago, the tears are flowing as they did April 13, 1996.

Kitty Man has visited me on a few occasions. One afternoon when I was cleaning the bathroom, I saw him coming down the hall just as he always had. I have also felt him jump on the bed while I was reading, and I have heard him meow. Before his death, when I read in bed in the late evenings, Kitty Man would join me. He would lie on my stomach and wait to be scratched.

I always feel comforted when he visits me or when he appears in my dreams. I know that he felt secure and loved all the time he was with me. I felt much pleasure and some pain, but the journey was so worth it.

Noreen

84

Mattie

She came into our lives in the aftermath of a hurricane. We found her in a park after two days of solid rain. Mattie was wet, dirty, and disheveled. She was looking for a place with some protection and looked so helpless that we rushed home to tend to her needs. She appeared to be a Golden Retriever and Chow mix, weighed about 65 pounds, and probably was 10 or 11 years old.

Mattie proved to be a special member of our family. She got along well with our cats and enjoyed being around other animals. She socialized well with people too.

She absolutely loved the cat's food and sneaked some at every opportunity. She was an imp at times, but you could not scold her when she looked at you with those endearing eyes of hers. Mattie had an unusual habit. She often winked at us. I had never seen a dog before that did this. She was sweet, well mannered, and loving.

One Sunday morning, a friend and I took her to the groomer's as was the usual routine. On this particular day, instead of leaving right away, I had a feeling of foreboding and felt that I must stay for a while. We stayed about an hour and then my friend suggested that we leave, which we did.

About two hours after I was home, the groomer called and said there was something wrong with Mattie. I ran from the house without my purse and shoes and drove over one hundred miles an hour to reach her. During the ride, I knew I should have stayed with her longer. I vowed the next time, I would go with my gut feeling.

When I arrived, I saw that she did not put any weight on her right front paw. The vet's clinic was open, and he took x-rays. The film showed a chipped elbow. I could have dealt with that, but further examination showed her entire leg was riddled with cancer. My dear Mattie had not acted as though she were ill. She had not limped, cried or complained. Still, I felt I should have known that she had a problem.

We discussed her condition, and I sadly learned there was no treatment or hope for her. There was no alternative but to keep her from more pain. It seemed that as fast as she had come into our lives, she was leaving.

I lay on the floor with her as the doctor injected the medication. I held and petted her until she drifted into her final sleep. I begged her to go with it, but she fought death to the end. After she was gone, I could hardly move. It was as though I had lost a child. Mattie was my child.

I thought back to the day that we found her in the storm. There must have been a reason that she was there for us. I wondered if we chose her, or she chose us. Whatever the reason, she brought so much to our lives.

After we returned home, the clinic called to ask what we would like to do with her remains. We chose communal cremation because she loved other animals so much. We felt that it would be her wish.

That night I prayed to God asking Him to show me a sign that Mattie forgave me for putting her down. That sign came three days later.

At first, I just dreamed about her. On Saturday when I was home alone, I heard a dog barking in my bedroom. It appeared to come from her favorite sleeping area. I waited a moment and heard it again. When I went to investigate, Mattie wasn't there.

That night I smelled her scent and felt her moving around. I just knew she was there. Next morning, I told my husband, and he felt I had lost it. I went to church again that morning, and prayed again for God to allow her to come to me.

It is the little things that make me believe. I fill the cat's food bowls in the morning, and when I come home from work the bowls are empty. My cats don't eat all the food in their bowls during the day. Her favorite napping place still has her smell. Some days her smell is gone, and then a few days later it is back again. After the carpets were cleaned, her scent was still there. I called the cleaning company and was told that a deodorizer had been used that eliminates any odor in the carpets, yet it returns again and again.

On one occasion, I was sleeping, and I heard her bark. Mattie rarely barked, so I got up to check out the noise, and she was sitting in the middle of the living room floor, wagging her tail like always, wanting me to give her attention. My heart leaped with hope at the sight of her, and then she was gone. I think she was telling me she forgave me for that wrenching decision. I believe she knew it was done with love.

After much grief, we got a new puppy. Mattie's visits slowed down for a short while. Our new puppy goes to doggy day care, and my neighbors downstairs tell me they can hear Mattie playing with the cats. Mattie, at 65 pounds, could not be mistaken for the cats running in the house. There was a strong bond between the cats and Mattie. It is just like her to visit them too.

I am grateful that she came into our lives, even though it was only for about two years. She crammed so much love into such a short time. I miss her so and treasure her visits to our family.

Heather Meyers

Mitzvah

In 1967, my wife and I were living in an apartment building in Queens, New York City. We returned home late one night and noticed a small black and white kitten waiting patiently between the inner and outer doors of the building. He appeared to be a mixed breed with big ears and a heart shaped face. We left him in the lobby, as we already had a cat and were not willing to adopt another on the spur of the moment.

When we saw him still waiting there the next day, we had a change of heart. He must have known that he was destined to be with us and was willing to wait as long as it took. We carried him upstairs, took care of him, fed him, and named him Mitzvah, which means "good deed" in Hebrew.

I soon learned that it was Mitzvah who did the good deed. He did us the favor of sharing our home. We had a very close relationship. In the evenings, after I settled into my recliner and later into bed, he would jump up to visit me with his head already in the proper position to rub against my face. He would then look at me with an intense expression, as if he were trying to understand me. He wasn't demanding, he was just content to spend time with me. Each of us was content to be with the other.

In 1973, we moved cross-country with our son, two cats, and a dog to California. Everyone adjusted quite well to our new home. Mitzvah was now allowed to venture outside but chose to remain in the yard. He seemed happy to be wherever we were. Each day when I returned home from work, he would come to greet me as soon as he heard my car.

One afternoon in 1982, I was being led through an exercise of guided imagery at the Unity Center in Walnut Creek, the subject of which was completely unrelated to pets or animals. Suddenly an image of Mitzvah, who was then 15 years old, walked into my consciousness. When I mentioned this to my therapist, she told me to make him welcome.

When I returned home that day, Mitzvah was not there to greet me. I later looked for him, and a neighbor told me that he was lying in the ivy bed. I found him in convulsions and immediately took him to the emergency hospital. The veterinarian told me that my beloved pet was near death and would not recover. There was no hope for him, and he was euthanized.

I related the incident at my next imagery session, and the therapist told me that Mitzvah had entered the session in order to say good-bye. He was faithful to the end. He chose to say his good-byes before he left our world.

I'm so glad that he chose me. Though this happened years ago, I still ache, but I'm comforted in the fact that he chose me. He was every bit a "Good Deed," my Mitzvah.

Mark R.

Leo

My husband and I seem to collect animals wherever we go. It isn't that we deliberately seek them out. I suppose, the animals find us. At this particular time, we have three horses that were rescued abuse cases. We also have five dogs, and three of them were abuse cases.

One pet, a bunny, stands out as a particularly favorite pet. We adopted Leo from the Humane Society, and he was a wise choice. I will keep him in my heart forever, and he will always be near me in spirit.

On a Saturday, we went to a Petco store where they were having an adoption fair. We found Leo huddled in his cage, surrounded by barking dogs, and looking like he really needed a friend. We took him out of the cage, and he just clung to us like glue – so we had no choice but to adopt him. Five dollars later, we were the proud parents of a four-year-old French Lop bunny with big brown eyes that would melt anyone. His fur was a rich fawn brown color and was as soft as could be. To take him home, we bought a cage and accessories for him, food, and treats too.

When we arrived home, he investigated everything and "chinned" things. That is what rabbits do to say, "This is mine." He chinned us too. They rub the underside of their chin on whatever they like and leave their scent on it (we can't smell it) to mark friendly territory. It's similar to cats rubbing against what they like. Rabbits also share the ability to be litter box trained.

We had never owned a bunny before, and we watched him to see how he was settling in. We saw that he was grinding his teeth. Not knowing if he was in pain, we rushed him to the emergency pet hospital to get him checked out. (New parents syndrome.) The vet examined him, and it turned out that he was grinding his teeth because he was happy! It's called "tooth purring." It's similar to a cat's purring to show contentment. We, being new parents, had no idea. Bunnies can grind their teeth when in pain also, so it still was worth checking.

Leo had some dog mannerisms too, such as licking my husband's face. He was very affectionate with both of us and adjusted well into our household. He showed his affection by giving bumps with his nose on our legs, face or nearest body part.

We settled into a routine. Play with Leo, go to work, come home and see what he had gotten into during the day, ...play with Leo, and so on. I spoiled him as rotten as I could, giving him fresh greens every night for dinner with plenty of carrots.

He had free movement in the apartment and found much to do. Most of it was amusing. One morning I found him in front of my jewelry box with all my treasures spread around him. I feel that he was trying to decide which bauble would be best for a toy. A frequent and fun activity was running around with a strip of newspaper in his mouth. It fluttered like a banner over his back as he ran from room to room.

Leo loved toys. A little stuffed bear was his favorite. He liked baby toys that made noise like rattles, keys, and cat toys like wire balls he could throw around.

When it was time for me to go to work, he would chase after me to give me a bump. He would steal the car keys from my purse, and I would have to give chase. How could he have known that without keys, I would have to stay home? As soon as I retrieved the keys, he would follow me down the hall, and I would have to shoo him back before he made an escape. He spent his days entertaining himself. Most of it was mischievous.

At bedtime I would rip up newspapers for him to sleep in a soft fluffy bed. He would make it up before he went to sleep. At night he would sometimes run around chasing us or sometimes sit like a quiet little doorstop, purring away.

Unfortunately, the time came when Leo became ill with an infection that was incurable. We, along with the vet, tried to make him comfortable the last year of his life.

One morning I awakened to find that Leo had passed away. It was a shock to find him with his paws together as if in prayer. He had a peaceful look on his face, and I felt that he hadn't been in pain when the angels took him. I mourned his passing.

Several days later, as I was on the sofa folding clothes, I felt the familiar bump – bump on my ankle. I was caught by surprise. I knew the cause of the bump but couldn't believe for a moment that it was Leo telling me he was there. We knew he loved us but was not quite ready to leave us.

The next few days, my husband and I heard the sounds of Leo running around the apartment. His audible trail rushed through the hall and behind our bed as he always had done. It was a comfort to me to have him near and made my grief a bit easier to bear.

Leo was such a special bunny, as I'm sure they all are if given the chance to develop their personalities and their relationships with people. We are grateful that someone brought him to the Humane Society. They must have had a legitimate reason to do so. I feel that it was so we could choose Leo, or he could choose us.

Betty S.

Native Dancer

Sometimes if you are very lucky, a soul mate comes into your life. That's what happened to me when Dancer chose me that day at the shelter. I needed him as much as he needed me.

He was with me for eight months before he was taken by lymphoma.

He made good use of his time with me. We took walks and had our own special fun places. Dancer, in his short life, accumulated 45 tennis balls, and even though he couldn't count, he seemed to know when a few were missing.

He adored my daddy and insisted he play ball with him each time he visited. Dancer nagged him by jumping, barking, and running to the back door to get his point across. Daddy would pretend he didn't understand, and Dancer would just have the "puppy crazies" until my dad would say, "Oh! You mean you want to play BALL? Is THAT what you want to do?" It was quite a trek to get all 45 balls out to the yard, but Dancer could cram several in his mouth at a time. That was part of the game. After a vigorous workout for both Dancer and Daddy, a time out had to be called.

When it was time for my folks to go home, Dancer would be frantic. He acted as though he wanted his people to be with him all the time. I discussed this with an animal communicator and was told that he felt he might not see them again and that is why he got so upset.

Dancer had a basketful of toys with very obnoxious sounds. Of course, his favorite time to play with them was about 2:00 a.m.! It was very disconcerting to be sleeping rather soundly and be awakened by a sound that closely resembled a duck! When I would "question" his choice of activity, he would sigh very dramatically ... then start to snore. Guys ... they are all alike!

At one time, I took Dancer to Washington National Cathedral for the annual Blessing of the Animals. It was a wonderful experience. We all sang "All Things Bright and Beautiful." The most joyous part was that all of the animals joined in on the chorus, stopped singing during the verses (I guess they didn't know the words), but re-joined the human voices each time the chorus came around again.

As the priests passed through the crowd, they individually blessed each animal, naming them and sprinkling them with holy water, just as is done at a christening. When the priest asked my dog's name, I said, "Dancer." The priest called him by name, at which point Dancer looked the priest right in the eye, accepted the sprinkling, and smiled back at him.

I believe that animals were given to us to teach us how to love, how to act unselfishly, how to be noble and true, and to reach outside of ourselves for the benefit of others. That is why it hurts so unbearably when we have to return these precious soul mates to their Maker, the Giver of Life, when they become so ill or infirm that we cannot make them well.

I think all creatures created by God have "souls." While we are the ones "created in God's image," we were given dominion over "the beasts of the field, the birds in the air, the fish in the sea..." to CARE for them as creatures made by the living God.

So as we are all "different," so must our souls, our essence, be too. Why would the time of peace and tranquility speak of the "lion lying down with the lamb..." unless it indicates in its very nature that these animals would be able to "sense" a difference in their relationship? Why would writers through the ages speak of the emotional bond, the saving of lives, the abilities to "sense" that our animals have, if not for their inner being – their souls?

British composer Benjamin Britten's Festival Cantata, "Rejoice in the Lamb," written on excerpts from an extended poem of the same name, "Jubilata Agno," consists of ten short sections, all dedicated to the glory of God in a manner somewhat foreshadowing poets Blake and Whitman. In it, names from the Old Testament are linked with various animals in the praise of God.

One of the most hauntingly beautiful sections, I think, is one I have had the privilege of singing and begins, "For I will consider my cat, Geoffrey. For he is the servant of the Living God, duly and daily serving Him. For at the first glance of the glory in the East, he worships in his way. For this is done by wreathing his body seven times round with elegant quickness. For he knows that God is his Savior. For God has bless'd him in the variety of his movements. For there is nothing sweeter than his peace when at rest. For I am possessed of a cat, surpossing in beauty, from whom I take occasion to bless Almighty God."

If the Beatitudes teach us that "Blessed are the pure in heart, for they shall see God" – then there are an awful lot of our pets now seeing God. For they ARE the pure in heart.

Dancer's blue water bowl still sits under the sink in the bathroom. The impression of it refuses to come out of the carpet, so I keep it there filled with water. It makes me feel better, so I really don't care what anyone else thinks of it.

I have had many visitations from him since his passing, and there is not a day that passes that I don't think of him or miss him terribly.

On the anniversary of his death, I decided I would take a walk on our favorite route. It was painful making the walk alone, but I felt it would help me remember some of our special times. When I reached the house of Dancer's friend, Provance, she ran to get a tennis ball for me to toss to her. She hadn't forgotten the routine.

Another memorable place was a patch of grass where Dancer would roll and play. I turned away and looked further down the street. I saw a man and woman with two dogs; one was a Spaniel, and the other could have been Dancer's twin. I could hardly breathe. As they neared, I knew that this was real and not a dream or wishful thinking. I knelt down on the sidewalk. The Spaniel continued to walk past me, and the other dog, Dancer's mirror image, walked into my outstretched arms and gave me a kiss. He then raised his head and looked deeply into my eyes. They too were Dancer's eyes and Dancer's smile. For just a moment, we were suspended in time right there on the sidewalk. For those who feel that animals can't be angels, they are wrong. I met mine that day.

I recognized what a precious gift I had been given. Just when I needed to hug him most, he was there for me again as he was before, and I now realize that he always will be.

I remembered the last time we visited his park, the day before I sent him home. He wanted so badly to play, but he simply had nothing left but the strength of his magnificent and loving heart. He lay down in the green grass that is spring and looked at me for a moment, then turned his head away. I took him home. The next day, when his doctor came to put him down, we were out in the front yard. He saw her get out of her car and woofed at her. She came into the yard, and Dancer brought her his stick. Dancer NEVER brought you a stick ... he teased you with it. Instead, he lay it at her feet.

Giving Dancer back was the hardest thing I have ever done. I held him in my arms and sang "The Dancer Song" to him as his vet mercifully ended his suffering. Then I handed him to God to heal him. For all he gave me, if the price of his wellness was that I had to give him back, it was a price I would willingly pay. But it was and is very hard.

I know he is safe. I know he is well. But he misses me, and I miss him. He does not want me to grieve, but he knows I will. I try not to because I know it makes him sad in the midst of his joy of health, and chasing bunnies, and butterflies, and staying out all night looking at the stars, and drinking "divine" water.

He comes to me in my dreams and sometimes sneaks into my room at night. Kind soul that he is, he sometimes brings friends who have had no human to truly love them. I told him that his friends are always welcome in my house, in my room, and in my heart.

I wrote this poem for Dancer.

Just This Side of the Moon
A blue water bowl sets under the sink
    waiting for Dancer to come take a drink.
But he will not visit anytime soon.
    His spirit now rests just this side of the moon.
A place cool and quiet, a place near the stars,
    a place where his body can heal all its scars.
A place calm and peaceful, a place with no noise,
    a place where he slumbers with all of his toys.
But one day his bright eyes will open anew,
    and if I know Dancer, he'll need something to do.
Perhaps, he'll take walkies or roll on the lawn.
    Perhaps, he'll see morning before it is dawn.
Perhaps, he'll go visiting all of his friends.
    If so, he'll be thirsty before the day ends.
Then he'll come and see me while out on the run.
    He'll stop in to tell me he's having such fun!
And off he will dash just as quick as a wink,
    but not before stopping to take a big drink
of crystal clear water. He can't get enough.
    His pink tongue a lapping that wonderful stuff.
Sweet pup, I'll be ready when you start to stroll.
    You'll know where to find it, that blue water bowl.
It's right where you left it — it's right where you think —
    waiting to meet you down under the sink.
So come when you're ready. I hope 'twill be soon.
    I'll see you come running from this side of the moon.

                          Susan

Nomi

She came to live with us when she was an eight-week-old puppy. Nomi was sold to us as a male. Lo and behold, that was not the case. She was a stubby-legged Dachshund and Beagle mix and quite adorable.

She was our first dog after our marriage. I was pregnant at the time, and Nomi was patient with me while I learned to care for her. It was important practice for me and the things to come. I hadn't trained a dog or cared for a baby before.

One of the things that made a big impression on me was that we had to teach her to follow a point. During a game of ball, Nomi didn't understand what we meant if we pointed or motioned in the direction of a toy. She finally made the discovery when she learned to follow my finger as I led her to an object. This, eventually, evolved into a game in which she would follow a trail.

As Nomi grew a bit older, she would run to the closet and wait while I put on my shoes. It isn't that I went around barefoot, but Nomi seemed to know that when we went out that was where the "traveling" shoes were kept. Her chances were good that she would be able to go with me, and it was important to her that she would be ready. It paid off as we often took her.

When Nomi was about nine years old, pretty much the average life span for her breed, we were faced with a move to Europe. We felt the move would be a difficult adjustment for her, and then she would have to face quarantine. She absolutely adored my mother, and it was decided that she would be happiest with her. We missed her a lot but knew it was best for everyone.

When Nomi was around 12 years old, she had a stroke. She was now blind and could no longer walk. It was with a heavy heart that my mother had her put to sleep.

Mother missed her terribly, but she told me she felt comforted knowing that Nomi was still near. She knew this because each time she vacuumed her plush carpet, paw prints would appear leaving an indentation. Mother would vacuum, and the prints would reappear. This continued to happen on a regular basis for several weeks, before it finally stopped.

You will never convince my mother that the spirit dies with the body.

Dee

Pax

On my 21st birthday, I visited the SPCA and gave myself the gift of Pax, a Miniature Schnauzer. He was destined to be the greatest gift I ever received.

He was between four and six weeks old and was placed at the shelter because his mother had died. It was necessary to feed him formula with an eyedropper supplemented with a bit of baby food. He was about four inches tall and weighed about one pound. Pax, which means peace in German, was from a litter of four, and I have always regretted that I hadn't taken two puppies.

Pax was one of the smartest dogs I have ever known, and I've had over 25 in my lifetime. He seemed to think he was a person and acted as such. We went everywhere together. My friends and family welcomed him to their homes, and he even went to work with me.

Riding in a car was a special passion of his, and he did lots of it. He stood and looked out the whole time and watched the scenery go by. You could tell by his actions, he knew where we were going. He quickly learned the route to every place we visited. I think that if he could have reached the pedals, he could have made the drive himself. He would always look stunned if we took a familiar route and didn't make an expected turn. He would look at us as if to say, "Hey, guys, you missed it!" He never missed spying his favorite landmark, the "Golden Arches," where he always got his own cheeseburger.

If it rained, Pax would chase the windshield wipers. He became totally frustrated when he realized that no matter how fast he followed them, he couldn't win this game. However, that didn't keep him from trying. He, most always, did whatever he set out to do. I ran fewer errands in rainy weather in deference to his inflated ego.

Pax knew when we were going to "Grandmas" or to the vet's office long before we got there. One he liked, the other he didn't. Grandma gave him special treats. Even though he loved Grandma (she always fed him good stuff), he didn't like to stay anywhere I wasn't. One time he scratched a hole through her sliding screen door because I had left him to run to the store. I was only gone an hour, but Mom said he was just beside himself, and she couldn't do a thing with him. Knowing what I know now, he was more attached to me than is good for a dog, but I loved it nonetheless.

We were so close. He slept on our bed. If he needed to go outside, he would stare at me to wake me up.

Fetching a ball or stick was his favorite game, and he would play to the point of exhaustion. Once during a game of fetch, with his eyes ever on the ball, he ran into a tree, flipped, landed on his feet, kept on going, and retrieved it with no time wasted.

We had other dogs during this time, but Pax was the top dog. Frequently, he would run to the back door and bark. When I opened the door, he'd stand to one side, all the other dogs would go running out, then Pax would go back in the living room and get on the couch. Apparently, he didn't think they belonged inside. He faked them out a lot! When he felt it was time for them to come inside, he would repeat his barking routine.

Pax was brave. He showed no fear of animals or people. At the age of ten weeks, he tried to take on two German Shepherds. Fortunately, I was there to run interference. He definitely disliked men in uniform and once bit a gas station attendant when he reached in to collect the money. Pax was protecting me. Luckily, the attendant understood he had invaded Pax's territory.

Once when a dog was abandoned near our home, we took him in. He evidently had been abused. The marks on his neck suggested he had been hanged. A trip to the vet showed a positive result for heartworm. The vet gave him the treatment for it and sent home a packet of tranquilizers to keep him calm. I carelessly left the packet on the coffee table. Pax disliked medication so much, I thought nothing of it. When any of the dogs were on medication, I would put a dab of peanut butter around the pill, and most of them readily took it. Pax would eat the peanut butter and spit out the pill. Perhaps he thought the newly found Hobo was getting too much attention and gobbled down all of the medication. It was three times a fatal dose for the little one.

During the night, I awakened to see Pax on the bed next to me literally shredding the sheets; then he fell unconscious. A few minutes later, he was shredding the sheets again. We rushed him to emergency, and he remained there for three days of IVs. I don't think he was so jealous that he tried to end it all, but my family still talks of the time when Pax "OD'd" on pills.

When Pax was over 17 years old, his hearing was impaired, and he was having trouble getting up and down the stairs. First, we carpeted the stairs to make it easier for him. If he fell, his fall would be cushioned. Even this grew to be too much, so we moved our bedroom downstairs. We did everything possible to help him cope with his limitations.

Around the age of 18, he no longer had any interest in all the things he had loved to do before. He was deteriorating much too quickly, and I had to make a decision. I agonized over it for some time, and then I finally made the appointment. I remember it so well. It was on Election Day, 1988.

I had a difficult time dealing with his death. We had two Schnauzers, one Poodle, and one mixed-breed dog. Even if you could have rolled them all together, you wouldn't have one Pax.

One night I awakened, and there was Pax staring at me. I sat up in bed to go see what he wanted. He turned and walked out the door.

His tail was wagging, and he had his favorite ball in his mouth. It took several seconds for me to remember that he was no longer with us. There is no doubt in my mind about Pax's visit. I have also seen him slipping out the back door with the other dogs.

He was by far one of the biggest and most important influences in my life. I have always felt that God resides in all of us, especially dogs. They only see the best in people, even in those who don't deserve it.

I will always have a special place in my heart for my Pax. He lived up to his name. He finally gave me peace.

Bonnie

Ringo

Ringo, or Rinks as I called him, came to me through a friend and her sister. They bred their dogs, and I was able to choose Rinks.

I drove 360 miles to fetch him, and every mile was worth it, as I was soon to learn. He was just a scrap of black and tan, but he was a handsome puppy. He was sedated for the long ride home to reduce the trauma of a first car ride and a long one at that. My poor Rinks had just had stitches removed from having his tail docked. I would have left him complete, but the deed had been done.

He was easily house trained and learned the commands to sit, stay, carry, and fetch. I could even place a biscuit on each front paw and tell him to "Leave." He wouldn't touch them until I said, "Fetch."

My husband, now my ex, wasn't happy because he didn't have a pedigree. I loved Rinks, as did my two children. I allowed them to choose his name, and it seemed to fit just fine. Rinks returned our love many times over.

His life was happy. Together we enjoyed walks, running, and chasing thrown sticks. However, one beach run proved to be a tragedy. Ringo had an artery cut from broken glass left on the beach. He was placed in the car, and I made a mad run to the vet. After several stitches, we all limped home.

Rinks wasn't accident prone, but he did have a few close calls. He was declared the town hero after one incident. It seems he lifted his leg on a lamppost and got an electric shock. He was so startled, he jumped up on a nearby wall and wouldn't come down. There was an electrical fault in the area. One farm nearby had "live" water taps in their kitchen. We phoned the police to report Rinks' misfortune, and the problem was corrected. It was felt that Ringo probably saved some lives there. It was written up in the Sunday papers here in the UK. Fortunately, Rinks wasn't injured, but I don't think he raised his leg very high for a few days. He didn't seem to be embarrassed by his claim to fame.

As time went on, the husband got worse, so I did the decent thing and invited him to be on his way. My father stepped in and took Rinks for his daily walks. (I worked every day.) It was good company for Rinks, and my dad got his exercise.

His absolute favorite treat was a bag of crisps (potato chips). You know how hard the bags are to open. Rinks would put his paws on the bag, push all the air to the top, nibble the corner of the bag, and rip it open, and help himself.

Time passed much too quickly. Rinks got older, and I didn't want to face that fact. He used to come up to the bedroom every morning to lie on my bed while I got ready for work. The time came when he had to be helped up the stairs. He would place his two front paws on the bottom stair and give out one soft "woof" to let us know that he wanted to come up.

For the last four years of his life, I went away on holiday at the same time each year. My daughter looked after him for the week I was away. That last year, I planned to leave July 19, 1997. My bags were packed, and I had planned to leave right after work. I rushed into the house to get a few last minute things done. While I was finishing up the chores, I noticed that Rinks had begun to pant. He jumped from his bed to the settee in a panic. His lips had gone very pale, and he just looked at me. The look that passed between us was as if he were saying, "This is it." He held my gaze, and the words just seemed to be there. I ran to phone the vet and for my dad to come. Rinks jumped from the settee to the floor and tried to get to me in the hallway. I grabbed a cushion for his head. My mum and dad were there within minutes. By this time, Rinks couldn't move. He looked up at my dad and whimpered. I lay on the floor close to him, held his head, and told him, "Go to sleep, my Rinks, before the vet comes." That was the most difficult sentence I have ever said. He died in my arms before the vet arrived. My dad reckoned that Rinks had chosen to die while I was with him. Dad had taken Rinks for his usual walk that morning. It was just a slow and leisurely stroll. It was a favorite time of day for him. The quality of his life was good. He was loved by so many people and made each of us feel special.

He had a long life for a large dog. The usual span for a dog his size is around 10 or 11 years, and Rinks was almost 13 years old. I am so grateful for those extra years that he was with me.

I decided I would go on holiday to see if I could get away from the pain. It didn't help. My grief was still felt but from a different location. It has now been two years since his death, and I still feel the pain. Rinks' collar still smells as if it has just been removed from his neck. I think our shared love knew no limits. At times, I think I have faced his leaving, and other times, I think not.

When I returned from Holiday, the house seemed so empty because Rinks was not there to greet me. There were times when I would hear the click of his toenails on the floor. I would look around to greet him and then realize that he is no longer here.

A year after his passing, I came out of the bathroom and tripped over him. Rinks would always lie in front of the bathroom door until I finished my bath. I saw him as I tripped, but then I seemed to trip over nothing but empty space. He'd gone just as quickly as I saw him. He continues to show up at emotional times in my life. Now and again, I hear just a slight noise at the foot of the stairs like a footfall. I've seen a flash just outside my bedroom door. Perhaps, he is there to offer support or comfort. I really don't know, but I feel he knows I still need him.

Another favorite place for him to lie was at the bottom of the stairs. He could keep track of everyone from this position. Once my daughter almost tripped over him at the landing.

I have good memories of our time together. When Rinks experienced his first snowfall, he would catch the flakes in his mouth. It would appear that he was biting the air. In the summer, he would catch the water from the hose in his mouth. It was obvious that it was a favorite game.

The picture that makes me smile is the one of Rinks lying on the settee with a bag of crisps clutched to his chest and resting between his front legs. Each time I open a bag of crisps, I think of my Rinks. He gave me so much pleasure, and I wish I could live it through all over again. He was my hero before he was officially declared one by our town. He didn't need to do a special deed. It was enough for him to be Rinks.

Meryl

Pretty Boy

When I was 11 years old, I had a wonderful horse. He was the first horse I had, and he was a Golden Palomino. He really deserved the name Pretty Boy, and he was destined to be my savior.

I was both sexually and emotionally abused by my father as I was growing up. When I was racing on the back of Pretty Boy or grooming him in the barn, I felt no one could reach me. For the first time, I knew freedom. This was destined to last for five years.

We were quite a team. We competed in shows and barrel events. In our last show together, we won first in a barrels class and second overall in versatility. The last show of the season, in August 1974, Pretty Boy came up lame.

When I was 15, I had a boyfriend who was "the special one." He was my first love and the one with whom I could spend the rest of my life. It was that same August that he was killed. My true love was gone, and all the hurts I had ever experienced surfaced. I was devastated.

It was only one month later, I learned Pretty Boy had brain damage and would soon have to be put down.

It was the next January that my dog was hit and killed by a car. When Pretty Boy had to be put down in May, I thought my life was over. Again, all the old hurts surfaced.

After a time, I was ready and needed another horse in my life. One summer night, I was out in the barn cleaning the stall of Burt, my new quarter horse. As usual, everything went smoothly, but then Burt began to act as though he was spooked. I tried to calm him, but he pawed the ground and shook his head. Burt had never done this before.

I finally looked out over the pasture and saw an image. It was Pretty Boy and David, my true love, was on his back. They stood there for the longest time, and it was as though they were telling me to go to my future. I was still watching as Pretty Boy and David disappeared into the night. At that moment, I knew they would always be by my side.

Over these past years, whenever things went wrong and seemed impossible to deal with, I felt Pretty Boy and David were at my side again to give me enough strength to handle the situation.

They are a reminder of the love they gave me. They are also a reminder that I am worthy of love. Animals really do help us heal the hurts that life deals out. During bad times, I am able to draw on the inner strength they gave me. My life has been enriched. My faith is more profound. I am so grateful that they came into my life, even briefly.

Vickie S.

Purrcey

Purrcey, a beautiful Siamese cat, was a year old when I met him at the Santa Clara County Humane Society. He was found in a trap somewhere in Mountain View, California. He was completely cat-a-tonic. He would or could not speak, move his eyes or respond in any way.

I adopted this gorgeous Siamese anyway. He reminded me of my first love, another Siamese, named Blubber, who had died some time ago. I often thought that Blubber came back to me as Purrcey.

I named him Purrcey because I knew that, ultimately, he would come around and respond to me. He was also named after the brave Round Table knight, Sir Perceval.

About six-months after I adopted him, he did come around and deigned to sit next to me and then finally on my lap, which he later never left. We were a matched set. I would park myself to watch TV, and he would watch me. Whatever I did, he watched me. His devotion was obvious.

We were able to spend more than 11 years together before he became ill. The look in Purrcey's eyes told me, I would not have him much longer. The final two weeks of his life, he refused food. It seemed that he was not ready to leave me.

A short time after he was gone, I would get a glimpse of him out of the corner of my eye. He was going into another room or dashing out of my view. His spirit lives on, and I am pleased that he remains with me.

Just as we have work to do while here on earth, so do our pets. My pets have taught me the meaning of courage, love, and best of all, their unflinching devotion and loyalty, all the qualities to which we aspire. I also feel that when they come back, they are showing us that love endures through death. Perhaps, Purrcey came to me for that reason.

If mankind listens, there is hope for our future as a species.

Chris

Mitzi

Mitzi was born in the back seat of a car, and that is only one of the reasons I felt she was special. We were made aware of the big event because my father worked for the man who found the litter. Dad called Mom and asked if we should choose one when they were old enough to leave their mother. Of course, we wanted one and chose a little Calico girl with long hair. When she was seven weeks old, my mom brought her home and named her Mitzi. She was orange, black, white, and beautiful with a pretty round face. Good homes were found for the rest of the litter.

Although her name was Mitzi, I also called her Sabrina and Serapina, but the only name she would answer to was Kitty. I was about seven years old at that time, and I had read a book that had a character named Sabrina. I thought the name was quite glamorous.

She liked to play fetch. I had never seen a cat play fetch before, but I had a little, red, plastic Indian figure, and she adopted it as her only toy. When I tossed it, she would run get it, then return it to me.

There was a place near us where you could buy tomatoes in large, wooden crates. She used to love hiding in them when they were empty. When she was in it, she acted as though she were invisible. Like most cats, she loved "being invisible."

Anything Dad ate, she ate, even oranges and watermelon. Occasionally, Dad would share a hamburger with her, and she ate the meat along with the lettuce and tomato. Other than that, Mitzi ate the usual canned cat food. She would shake it to "kill" it before she ate it. The walls were always spattered with her food.

Mitzi seemed to favor Dad. She used to wait patiently for him to come home and sit in his chair. She would get in his lap and "make bread" (knead) until she was comfortable; then she would sleep.

When I went to bed, she joined me and chewed on my bookbindings while I read. When it was time for sleep, Mitzi turned in circles and flopped down in her own special place at the foot of the bed or on my pillow.

She often visited the neighbors and even followed me to school. Once, Mom had to come get her. She liked to go for walks in the neighborhood with my mom. Mitzi was a social little thing.

At one time, around the 4th of July, she was gone for a week. I didn't know back then, that so many pets run away because of the noise of fireworks. Had I known, I would have kept her inside.

Mitzi was hit by a car and killed when she was seven years old. I carried so much guilt over that. She had been asleep, and I wanted to play with her. She wasn't in the mood to play and asked to go outside. The car hit her as she ran across the street. After I grew up and owned cats, they were never allowed outside. I thank Mitzi for teaching me that lesson.

For weeks after her death, Mitzi visited me every night. I felt her circle around several times and then lie down on the bed. I told her every night that it was OK. She finally went on ahead to Rainbow Bridge, where all beloved pets wait for their owners. I never spoke of her nightly visits for fear I would be locked up. I found out many years later, after I had moved out and my parents moved into what had been my room, that Mitzi continued her nightly romps on their bed. My mother never noticed it, but my dad did. He accused my deceased grandmother of being the night visitor, but I corrected him.

I was fortunate to have spent many years with my dad. After his death, I have had the feeling that he is pulling the bed covers up around me, even though there is no visible movement. At these times, I also feel something move on my pillow. At first, I thought it was my present cat, but he wasn't there. I then knew it was Mitzi accompanying Dad on his visits.

The night my father died, I woke up at the time of his passing, about five minutes before the phone call came to tell us of his death. Other family members in a neighboring state awakened at the same time too. I have to believe that something special happened, and he is well and with several of my animal friends.

I feel that Mitzi and my other pets that have passed over are at Rainbow Bridge. Perhaps my dad checks on them there as well. I find comfort in believing that. This way, my loved ones are always with me. I know they are in my heart, and their spirit is near.

Owning pets over the many years has helped me overcome the fear of death that I had growing up. Mitzi helped me come to a feeling of acceptance several years ago. I wonder if she knew just how much love and comfort she gave me. Thank you Mitzi.

Sue Stange

Mitzi

It is hard to do justice to a pet you have loved. My cat, Mitzi, has always had a special place in my heart.

When she came into my life, I was married to a man who hated cats. In his younger years, he said that he liked to shoot them with his BB gun. Imagine my surprise when he returned home from a large department store with a tiny kitten. There had been two little girls in front of the store with a box of kittens. Mitzi, which we subsequently named her, must have made a connection with him.

Our apartment complex allowed no pets, so we had to keep her our secret. Later we got another cat, Peepers, to keep Mitzi company. Mitzi needed a companion to play with, and this worked out well.

Six months later, the owner of the apartment saw Mitzi and Peepers in an upstairs window. He barreled over and demanded that we get rid of both of them.

At the time, my husband worked with a nice, young man named Eric. Eric loved cats and had recently lost his own, so he agreed to take them both.

In those days, we were knot-heads and didn't realize how important it is to spay and neuter pets. Shortly after their move to Eric's place, they both became pregnant. After the birth of their litters, Mitzi settled in and became an excellent mother. Peepers had no interest in her kittens, so Mitzi adopted them as her own.

Mitzi was a pretty little thing. The young girl who gave her to us said she was an Angora. She had a long black coat that touched the ground in the winter months. Her "tuxedo" front was white on the chest and continued up to her mouth. This gave her a quirky and defiant look. Her whiskers were long and white, and her eyes were large and yellow, like those of an owl or an eagle.

We kept one of the kittens from Mitzi's first litter. He was a handsome boy and looked like the male on the block behind us. We named him Thunder. When Mitzi had a second litter, Thunder nursed along with the newborns.

Little did I know, I would soon be following Mitzi to Eric's home. Less than a year later, my husband informed me that he was in love with someone else.

As our marriage ended, Eric's relationship with his girlfriend ended also. At my husband's suggestion, Eric and I got together for a date. We've been together ever since. I had a problem at first with our relationship. There was a slight age difference, but I soon learned it didn't matter. I moved in and out a few times before I finally surrendered to the fact that we were meant to be together. Meanwhile, Mitzi endured my moves and finally enjoyed riding in the car. She was my constant companion during those trying times.

At one point, during a separation from Eric, I tried dating someone else. He could not tolerate Mitzi at all. Each time he came over, she would plant herself between us. When I didn't object, he became infuriated. It didn't take me long to figure out, I liked Mitzi and Eric's company much more than his.

Just as Eric and I had reached our happiest of times, Mitzi was killed. This happened a couple of years after we settled into our new home. Even Mitzi was more contented than she had ever been.

The day Mitzi died, Thunder ran into the house shaking all over and hid behind the television set. He only did that this one time. I thought there might be a strange dog in the neighborhood, so I brought Mitzi in to keep her safe. She seemed to sense my panic, and it scared her. She jumped from my arms and ran out the back door before I could close it.

I thought that maybe I was overreacting and went to take a bath. A short while later, Eric rushed in and said Mitzi was dying on the front lawn. A car must have hit her, and she was paralyzed. We tried everything in our power to help her, but we did not succeed. She tried to live, but the battle was lost after a week.

We buried her in a beautiful place where we had gone numerous times. We thought she would be safe there. It took months for Eric and I to come to terms with her death. Every year or so, we would go visit her gravesite. The day we buried her, we saw an eagle. On all our previous trips before Mitzi's death, we had never seen one there. I feel the eagle is there because he watches over Mitzi, and her spirit is in him. Her eyes were like those of an eagle, and perhaps, she chose him to help her spirit soar. This comforts me. Each time the eagle appears, it is to remind me that Mitzi's spirit is forever free.

Paulette

Maggie

I had been looking for a special dog for such a long time. It didn't have to be a particular breed, but I knew that I would recognize it when I saw it. Finally I went to the SPCA. When I went in, I entered the room where the puppies were kept in cages. They were jumping and barking except for one who was a mixture of Greyhound and German Shepherd. This little female was just quietly lying there. I put my hand up to her cage, and she licked it. From that moment on, I knew she was the one. We made a connection in those few seconds.

When I asked to take her, I was told she wasn't available because someone had called in and asked about a dog fitting her description. If she were still there at 5:00 p.m. the next day, she would be mine.

I was devastated. I don't know why the visit affected me so. On the way home, I saw a deer in a field. It reminded me of the puppy. When I arrived home, I went to my room for the rest of the night and didn't say another word.

The next day, some friends and I were in my basement. I needed to be distracted for the rest of the day until 5:00 p.m. During the prolonged visit, the front door opened and a very timid, 14-week-old dog peeked into the room. She was the special one from the SPCA. At that moment I said, "Her name is Maggie." The name was pulled out of the air, but I knew it suited her. My friend had gone to the shelter and picked her up a bit early, since the person who inquired about her had released her.

Maggie was light tan in color. Her eyes were very wise looking, lined in black, so they looked as if they had been lined with kohl. Her coloring along with the Greyhound influence made her look almost deer-like. When I looked into those eyes, I saw her beautiful soul.

In my senior year, in my advanced biology class, our teacher wanted us to do a dog intelligence test with our pets. The highest score was ten. Maggie got a ten, of course, and no other dog came close to her score. She was so smart that anytime you mentioned the words "park," "walk," "car" or "Daddy's hiking shoes," she would get excited. We had to resort to spelling those words in front of her. Eventually, she also understood the spelling for most of them.

Maggie was very tuned in to my moods. If I were feeling badly or sad, she could sense it and would lick my hand. One night I was lying in bed and thinking of something that really depressed me. I wasn't crying or showing any outward signs of grief. Maggie, who had been lying at the foot of the bed, got up from her spot, lay next to me, snuggled for a moment, and gave me a few kisses. After she felt that she had comforted me, she returned to the foot of the bed. It was her way of saying that everything was OK, and I wasn't alone. If I cried, she licked away the tears.

Some of my best memories of her were at Christmas time. I always bought her special presents. My mom and I would wrap all the gifts in her room. Maggie would lie outside, in front of the door. All the gifts I purchased for Maggie would be piled in my room. She was like a small child in anticipation of Christmas. Every day she would go into my room, stare at the pile of presents, lie down and cry. A couple of times, she just couldn't wait and sneaked a couple of them out of my room. When I noticed they were gone, I started searching. When I found Maggie, she was under the table with a still-wrapped gift in her mouth and was wagging her tail.

She enjoyed Christmas so! When the day finally came, Maggie gently opened her gifts very slowly and deliberately. You would think she was saving the wrapping paper so she could use it again. She was a joy to watch.

We had special times together. She enjoyed riding in the car because it usually meant going to our special place near the creek. There was a large and bent tree near the water that served as a bench. I sat there and watched Maggie play. In the excitement, she would jump around and bite at the water.

For five years, she had the undivided attention of everyone around her until my brother and his fiancé came by with Jamie, a tiny bit of fur with a big head. The puppy was an American Staffordshire Terrier. Maggie was crushed. She wasn't the center of attention and acted as though she were jealous. She tried to ignore the new puppy. It was really an act though, as she could be a real drama queen. Wouldn't you know? ... Jamie adored Maggie. She wanted to play with Maggie's toys, but if she touched one, Maggie would take it away and hide it. I babysat Jamie a couple of times a week, and I had hoped the two pets would become friends.

Each time Jamie was around, Maggie became very clingy. She was my shadow the entire time Jamie was there. Maggie would put on this "poor me" act, sit next to me, and heave a sigh. At the age of eight, she had perfected her act and was a real professional. It was only when Jamie was around that Maggie appeared to be old and helpless.

At one time, Maggie had injured her ankle, and of course, we made a big fuss about her boo-boo and commiserated over her misfortune. She was treated as though she were a princess. Now she used that experience — big time. When Jamie was over, Maggie would suddenly become lame. As smart as Maggie was, her memory failed her as to which foot was previously injured. She would limp on her right foot, but later in the day, she switched to her left. I always gave her extra attention when she did this, and of course, it reinforced her performance. It was shameless on my part, but I really appreciated the effort she put into her act.

Maggie really did like Jamie. If we were not nearby, she played nicely with her as if she were the big sister, and of course, the top dog.

I often took the two of them to the park where they could safely run off leash. This field was our special spot. Once Jamie turned renegade and ran away with me trailing behind. Maggie joined in to catch her, and I was getting frustrated. Maggie could really run, of course, as she was part Greyhound, and she tackled her for me.

Even though Maggie acted as though she wasn't fond of Jamie, she would pout each time Jamie went home. After Jamie left, Maggie would mope around for a day. She had her own special sulking spot between the couch and an end table. She would lie there and sigh deeply for hours.

Maggie's death was one huge surprise. She had never shown any signs of progressive illness. She acted extremely healthy and energetic on Christmas day in 1997. As usual, she had a blast opening all her presents and playing with her new toys.

I took her with me as I drove around with my ex-boyfriend to look at all the Christmas lights. Maggie was in the rear of my station wagon looking out the rear window, as if she were saying goodbye to everything.

After I dropped my ex off, she had her back to me and continued to look out the window all the way home.

We went directly to bed and Maggie lay at the foot of the bed in her usual spot, but she wouldn't go to sleep. She started staring out the window and crying. I thought it was just too much excitement for the day. About a half-hour later, she jumped off the bed and vomited. I cleaned everything up and we went to bed again. I said a prayer to God to let her feel better. I remember pressing a scapular (a garment worn by some Roman Catholics as a token of religious devotion) and a Saint Anthony of Padua chaplet (a string of prayer beads) to her head. At the time, I didn't really know why I did that, but I had a strong impulse to do it.

She got sick again, and I took her downstairs to the kitchen to offer her water, but she wouldn't take a drink. I sat on the floor, and she buried her head on my chest. She always did that when she was upset. I just hugged her.

I didn't want her to stay downstairs alone on Christmas night, so we returned upstairs to bed.

When I awakened the next morning, my mom had already taken her downstairs and let her outside. When I looked out the window, I saw Maggie lying under our oak tree and sniffing the air. She looked very peaceful and happy. Before I went to work, I gave her my usual hug, as I always did on a normal day. She stared me in the eye with her usual, soulful look and gave a sigh.

My first patient that day was a doctor, who happened to be the father-in-law of Maggie's first vet. I bragged about how wonderful and intelligent Maggie was. I called Mom to see how Maggie was doing and was told that she was fine. I continued to my next appointment. This patient had to go for a dialysis treatment, and I drove him home. On the drive home, I saw the most beautiful clouds over the Philadelphia skyline. There were streams of sunlight peeking through the clouds and pouring over the skyscrapers.

My dad came to pick me up around 5:00 p.m., and on the way home Dad got a page from Mom while I was talking about Maggie. I had an unexplained feeling of dread. I returned the call on the cell phone and she said, "Just put Dad on the phone." All Dad said was, "What?" and I started screaming and bawling, "My baby. My baby."

I just knew that Maggie was gone. She had died about a half-hour earlier as I was watching the beautiful sun stream through the clouds.

I had to be held when I got home and went down the basement stairs where Maggie had been placed. My lifeless little Maggie was lying on her blanket. I just couldn't handle it one bit. This was the only time Maggie wouldn't lick my tears away. I held her close for the longest time. My parents left me alone with her, so I could say goodbye. I sang "On Eagle's Wings" to her. I had sung this to her so many times in the past and told her not to be afraid as there were so many people waiting for her. One of my brothers was waiting there with our previous pets and a friend's daughter. I told her I would never forget her, and she would always be my sweetheart. I promised her I would always take care of animals for her. I told her repeatedly how much I loved her. I wrapped a rosary around her collar, and my dad attached several of my Saint's medals including one of Saint Francis, the patron saint of animals. Late that night, I covered her with a beach towel so she would stay warm.

My brother and his fiancé came to say their good-byes. My mom went to the car to stay with Jamie. We didn't know how she would react if she saw a lifeless Maggie. When Mom got in the car, Jamie sniffed her like crazy, gave Mom a sad look, and began to cry. She seemed to know what had happened. I feel that animals grieve over another's death. They have many of the same emotions we have. They feel sadness, hurt, grief, and mourn as we do. They are too smart not to be aware of those things.

The next day, we took Maggie to be cremated, and this was done along with her favorite toys and her new leash that she got for Christmas. At first I wanted to keep her collar, but Maggie always hated it when her collar was removed. The rosary and medals were still fastened to it and a jingle bell that she wore at Holiday time. It began to snow. Maggie liked to play in the snow. I felt comforted.

A few days after Maggie's death, my brother brought Jamie over for a visit. Her normal routine was to first stop at the pantry for a treat. This time she ignored everyone and went directly to the basement, to the spot where Maggie had passed and began to cry. It was amazing and very sad. To this day, you cannot say Maggie's name around her, or she will cry. It really gets to me.

I was so damn lonely. I'm not one to live without animals in my life, so my mom and I visited the Humane Society. I spoke to Maggie in my thoughts and told her to give me a sign if there was a dog she wanted us to bring home. I kept thinking, "Maggie, give Mommy a sign."

When we passed by one cage, there was a shy little puppy just sitting there looking lonely and depressed, as Maggie had eight years earlier. All around her were noisy jumping puppies. I put my hand up to the cage, and she came and kissed it. I said to Maggie, "Is she the one?" Just then, the little puppy pushed a toy outside of the cage, looked at me, and wagged her tail. She reminded me of Mags.

My mom got the attendant so we could meet with the puppy in a room that is reserved for this purpose. If the meeting goes well and is approved by the Society, then, and only then, are you allowed to adopt.

We were told the puppy we asked to see was from an abusive home. Their concern was how she would interact with other people. If the pup didn't come to us, we would not be allowed to take her home.

As we waited for the attendant to bring the pup, both my mom and I asked for Maggie's help. If this wasn't THE puppy she wanted for us, don't let her come, but if she was, let her be eager to come. As the little one entered the room, she ran to me and gave me a kiss on my nose. She then picked a toy and took it to my mom. Everyone, including Maggie, approved of us. We named her McKenna. She had a look of Maggie about her. She has some of the same markings on her shoulders that are little light patches of fur. Maybe that is the place where the angel wings go. She is now 91 pounds and is part German Shepherd, Golden Retriever, and Rottweiler. She is about twice the weight Maggie was, but since Maggie helped pick her, she must have felt I could handle her. I now know she chose wisely.

I feel Maggie and I are still tuned in to each other. One of the signs that convince me of this is a song Janet Jackson recorded, called "Together Again." It speaks of seeing a loved one again in Heaven and they are looking down on you. Well, there are times when I'm thinking of Maggie, turn on the radio, and the song is playing. There is a field where Maggie liked to watch grazing deer, and I associated them with her. A few times the song has come on the radio as I'm driving by and see the deer. I feel Maggie is telling me that she loves me still, and she is fine.

One of the most remarkable moments came when I was at work. I had a Nun as a patient that day. I was taking care of her overnight at the convent. The convent is next to Maggie's favorite park. At night the deer come out and graze next to the building. While my patient slept, I walked out onto the balcony to look at the deer and check out the stars. It was a clear night, and I started to sing "Together Again." It had been playing in my head all day. I saw a brilliant shooting star as I was thinking of Maggie. I said to her, "Maggie, if that was you, can I have another shooting star?" A minute later, another star shot across the sky. I kept singing the song. I was amazed that I saw so many. I stopped singing to say thank you to my little baby. Then another star shot by.

Maggie seems to use shooting stars, that special song ("Together Again"), and deer to communicate with me. I believe this in my heart. There could never be that many coincidences. I truly believe.

After her death, the first time I visited her favorite spot by the creek, I tossed some flowers onto the water. I talked to her in my mind, and I swear I felt a breeze around me each time I said something to her. I always feel a sense of peace in that spot. I can feel her presence.

There are times when I have felt sad, and a dog would pass by that resembled her in some way to lift my spirits. Just the other day, when I was driving home with my fiancé, I saw a guy walking a dog who was a spitting image of my Maggie. I pointed out that fact to him. At that very moment, the dog looked straight at me. It's not just coincidence. I know. I believe.

Jenn

Max

My family and I always had a dog as a pet. When I was on my own, I had Poodles and later Shepherds. I grew up thinking that I probably wouldn't like cats.

After 16 years of living alone, I met my significant other. We were together for a short time when Max adopted me. He's what I call a Halloween cat, all black with yellow eyes and a misshapen ear. He was pre-owned by a tenant a couple of doors down the hall. The man was your average nice guy, until he drank. When he had consumed too much alcohol, he would stumble home at night and leave Max outside to fend for himself.

I was concerned about Max, and I felt that he deserved a better life. He was probably around 10 years old at that time. He began to wait for us to come home, and as soon as he heard our car, he was there to greet us. In my eyes, he was already my cat. For some reason, Max and I just clicked. I couldn't believe how much we were becoming attached to each other. (I think Max knew a sucker when he saw one.) He had been passed around in this small community before residing with his former owner from whom I "stole" him. He graciously donated Max's toys to me.

About this time, I was laid off at my job, and I stayed home for about six months and had a real pity party. Max would jump up on the bed and keep me company while I adjusted to my new situation.

He seemed to know that I needed him as much as he needed me. He was a great comfort to me, and we spent some good times together. At times, I felt Max knew that we were destined to be together.

After we had him for about four or five years, he developed a serious kidney problem. He had extensive treatment at the vet's office for about five days. When I brought him home, he didn't seem very happy. He recovered, but his health was never quite the same after that first illness. Still, he was able to run and function normally for the next year.

Max was not interested in food towards the end of his life and even turned down his favorite meal. I fixed him chicken breasts for special treats. I tried to entice him into eating and put baby food on my finger. He would lick off a bit and then finally eat the chicken but not enough to regain his strength. His condition deteriorated. He reached the point where he couldn't jump up on my bed to sleep in his usual place. I realized that he didn't care to go on, and I made his final appointment with the vet.

I know I made the last years of his life more comfortable than he could ever have been with the other tenant — and maybe, he knew that. Animals can be pretty savvy creatures. I tried to take comfort in the fact that his last years were spent in a loving home.

A short time after his death, there was what I thought to be a small earthquake in the night. The next night, it happened again, and it felt like Max was jumping up on the bed and then walking gently across or near my legs. I realized then that it could only be Max. For a while, it happened fairly frequently, sometimes several times in one week. It continues to happen even now but not as often. I believe that now he comes at significant times for me.

I tried to talk to a woman at work about Max's visits, but it only gave her the creeps. After that, I just kept it to myself. If Max wanted to visit me, then I was comforted by the fact that even though I had put him to sleep, he still loved me and wanted to be with me.

One day there was mention of similar events in the newspaper. I then confided Max's visits to my significant other. Much to my surprise, even though he pooh-poohs the paranormal, he admitted that he too had felt Max's paws and legs on his pillow, and that there was an impression left where Max would have lain on it. I was amazed, because he hadn't believed in that sort of "stuff."

Max is buried at a pet cemetery in Napa, California. I am not able, even now, to go visit his grave. I must resolve a few issues before I do. I think I was closer to him than I had ever been to any of my other animals. I had thought that this type of phenomenon happened to those who had a pet for many years. Now I think it may be the strength of the connection, instead of the length of time. I don't know why, I just know it is special. Whatever the reason, I'm pleased that Max cared enough to visit me. His visits gave me insight into the relationship that we had, and I treasure that.

Lynne

Punkin

Punkin came to us when she was about six weeks old. My daughter named her that, as she was a little, orange ball of fluff. A coyote killed her mother, and Punkin was the smallest of the liter. She had to be bottle-fed for about two weeks. One night she had to be watched closely because we thought that she was going to die. She pulled through by her sheer determination.

Punkin was very much a girl. She was very prissy, feminine, and had a sweet disposition. She spent much time preening herself and keeping herself clean. When we gave her a bath, she would scream her head off as though she were being mistreated. She was never one for rough play, so we treated her very gently. Her favorite game was chasing a laser dot flashed on the carpet. She would chase the dot until she gasped for breath. She may have related that to chasing prey. Though she had a reserved attitude, I think her wild nature came out when she played with the laser dot.

Her palate was a bit unusual for a cat. She hated bugs and chicken livers but loved kitty treats. It was easy to call her home. All I had to do was shake the can of treats.

Punkin was born outside, and she spent most of her time in the back yard. She was allowed to come and go as she pleased. She seldom ventured to the front of the house. That is why I was so shocked when a car hit her on the main street. My kids were devastated. We held a funeral in the rain for her, and she was buried in the back yard that she loved so much.

Every morning when she was with us, our routine was the same. I was always the first one to the kitchen to feed Punky and then let her outside.

After her death, I heard her crying for her breakfast in the kitchen. This continued for several days. I would automatically start to go to the kitchen to feed her, and then realize that she was no longer with us. We were all very saddened and missed her so much. It was a comfort to know that she was still with us in spirit for a while.

Robin Loggans

Sam

Sam was five months old when he came to live with my husband and me. He was the largest puppy in the litter. Sam was a registered Shih Tzu. Because of his size and a minor abnormality, he was not show material. But what did I care? We loved him exactly the way he was.

He was house trained and had only one accident in the house the entire 15 years time that he lived with us. That was my fault. When I first brought him home, I forgot to allow him to "go" before I took him into the house.

His temperament was gentle. He never snapped at anyone or anything. Once our Cockatiel pecked his nose. Sam thought about snapping; I could see it in his face, but he just backed away. I thought that was amazing.

His favorite toy was a ball inside a sock. I would toss it for him, and he would fetch it. Sam would get a treat when he returned it to me. The treat was placed on my knee, and he had to wait until I said it was OK for him to take it. We stopped playing this part of the game when Sam lost his hearing, as he was unable to hear the command. It was heartbreaking to see him just continue to sit — waiting to hear the "OK."

I thought Sam was brilliant. He could count to two! His treats were always given in sets of two. He then knew that was all. If he was given just one, he looked around for the other. Of course, he was never disappointed.

Sam loved to play with cats too. They weren't very enthusiastic about it, but he tried. He had such a good heart that he seemed to love everyone. He didn't do a lot of tricks and wasn't a rocket scientist. He was just our little boy, and we loved him so much.

He was my guardian angel and very protective of me. He was at my side when I arose in the morning and stayed by me until I went to bed. If I stayed up later than his dad did, he would sleep in the room where I was until I went to bed. He was "my" dog. He loved his daddy, but I was his leader or "Alpha," or come to think of it, I guess he was my Alpha too.

We had to send him to Rainbow Bridge when he became very ill. He was then 15 years old, and he had received as much love as we could give him his whole life.

I longed for him to return and went through some very sad times. Two days later, I heard him bark in the back yard the way he did when he was ready to come back in the house. Mothers can recognize their child's voice amid many others, and the bark I heard was unique to my Sam.

I was devastated. It just tore me up that first time. When it happened two more times a couple of days apart, I felt comforted.

I had thought that when he was gone, I would never "have" him again, but I did. I have not heard him again, but the pain is better now, and I think of him with love instead of so much grief.

Patsy E.

Ubu

Ubu was eight weeks old when she captured my daughter's heart at the Arts Fair in Los Gatos, California.

We lived some distance away but felt that she would not object to the car ride home. As it happened, she tolerated it. It was years later that she hated riding in the car and would shiver as she hid under the seat. She never preferred our company if it meant having to ride somewhere — especially when it was a visit to Grandma's fur-faces, Ubu's extended fur-family.

We knew she was going to be a very special cat, and we anguished over finding the perfect name for her. She was a black and white beauty, a Norwegian Forest Cat. Eventually, almost in desperation, I made up the name Ubu. That is what I thought anyway. I learned much later, there was a French playwright, poet or actor around the seventeenth century named Ubu. So much for originality.

But Ubu was totally original. As a kitten, she and I used to play hide and seek. It was Christmas time when she developed this game, and her favorite place to hide was under the Christmas tree skirt.

Her most endearing trait was to tuck me in every night when I went to bed. She would follow me upstairs and sit at the foot of the bed and groom herself as I did my nightly ritual. After I got into bed, she'd jump up and curl up beside me. Ubu stayed there only until she thought I was asleep, and then down she jumped and left the room.

Ubu knew she was a family member and was secure in the love she received. We were devastated when she was stricken with liver cancer at age 13. She had been mildly sick for a long time, but we didn't know it. She didn't show it, noble that she was.

The day after we buried Ubu, we visited my mother. She has two cats, one of whom is a real grouch. At one time, he was very affectionate, but I guess age turned him into a curmudgeon. During the visit, he came to me, let me pet him, and sat on my lap. He had always ignored me before. Perhaps, he sensed my grief, and it was his way of offering me comfort. It reminded me of Ubu sitting on my lap two weeks before her death. She had always preferred to be near us but not on our lap.

Our family was grief-stricken at her passing. I thought it was strange that I didn't feel her presence after she was gone. Then, one night, she came to me in a dream or vision. She sat on my lap and purred for a long time. The dream was so vivid and sensory that when I awoke, I was surprised she wasn't curled up next to me purring. It took a few minutes to realize that it must have been a dream. Perhaps, she will make another appearance. It would be appropriate for her to come back for an encore.

Dee

Sparky times Three

My mother grew up outside of Edison, New Jersey. When she was about eight years of age, the family dog had puppies. One of the pups was a black-haired mutt they named Sparky. When Sparky was about a year old, she was out exploring a swamp with the kids. No one knows exactly what happened, but Sparky returned home with the kids that night with part of an eye missing. The vet felt as long as the eye remained uninfected, Sparky would be fine. Sparky (number one) lived for another 12 years, a loyal family member until the end.

Fast-forward 30 years to 1989. It was a cold winter at my parent's small family farm in Montana with the wind chill dropping the temperature to around 70 degrees below zero. I went outside to check on a flock of ewes that were very pregnant. I saw my horse, Starr, running around the flock of sheep and then noticed a little lamb half-buried in the snow. Her mother was trying to clean up the little one. I rushed over and picked up the lamb, intending to bring it to the barn. When I looked down, I saw the lamb had been bitten or stepped on by Starr, and one eye was out of the socket. I was so shocked, I dropped the lamb. I rushed to get my mother who then brought the lamb into the house. She put it near the wood stove to thaw out the poor baby.

My father inspected the tiny frozen one. He felt the lamb was beyond hope, and the kindest thing to do would be to mercifully end her suffering. He moved the lamb outside. When he returned with his rifle, the little one, remarkably, stood up and tried to nurse off a nearby barrel. My father decided, she was telling us that she wanted to live. We took her to the vet, and he removed the eye and stitched the lids closed. (Starr has never been with the sheep again.) Massive doses of antibiotics were given to her to treat the abscesses she developed from her injuries.

We named this little lamb Sparky in honor of the first Sparky my mom owned years before. The lamb, Sparky (number two), had a rough beginning. She had seizures from the head trauma she suffered in her encounter with Starr. The seizures continued her entire life.

Sparky lived in the house for 28 days. She bonded with her human family and followed us everywhere. She didn't like to sleep in the box I had prepared for her, so I spent those 28 days sleeping on the couch or floor with her. Sparky awakened me for her 2:00 a.m. and 4:00 a.m. feedings. Luckily for all of us, eventually, she was able to recover enough to move into the barn and learn how to be a sheep. I missed her terribly.

Sparky was always given special treatment and became spoiled. If we were late when it was time to feed the animals, Sparky protested by bleating loudly. She voiced her displeasure loud enough that she could be heard inside the closed house.

At a later time, when she was first bred, she delivered twins. One eye was a distinct handicap. It was difficult to keep track of two babies. From then on, she had a single birth each year. She was aware of her limits.

In Sparky's last year, she had a little ewe, and we named her Mary. That isn't an original name for a lamb, but it suited her. Sparky became ill shortly after Mary's birth. Even with our veterinarian's attention, she died at the age of seven. Her passing devastated me. I would look out at the flock of sheep, and I would see her in the field. As I looked harder, I would see a different sheep. This was repeated many times. I feel it was her way of telling me she was still around and that it wasn't an optical illusion.

A year passed. I finally grew accustomed to the absence of her greeting me in the mornings. At this time, I worked at a children's shelter. It was always a treat for the children to go on an outing to the Humane Society. I usually didn't visit the dogs, as I am unable to look into those eyes and then leave the dogs behind. On that particular day, I decided to follow some of the kids into the kennel area. As we walked down the last isle, I passed a cage that held a Standard Dachshund. The first thing I noticed was that he only had one eye. When I saw this, the thought of Sparky's experience overcame me. The second thing I noticed was that his name card said, "Sparky." I stood there for a moment in disbelief. Sparky sat there, rather pathetically, in his kennel.

As soon as I could return home, I told Mom of the little one-eyed dog named Sparky. The next day, she went to see him, but the Humane Society had closed for the evening. We both returned the following evening, but Sparky was out visiting nursing homes. Finally, on a Saturday, we went to see him again. We then decided that it was fate, and Sparky (number three) came to live with us.

We learned that Sparky had been abused in the past. This caused some hardships for me when we first brought him home. He was destructive and sneaky. He could not be left alone for even five minutes due to his separation anxiety. With my veterinarian's advice, I crate trained him, and he has made progress.

Sparky's favorite things to do are eat, eat some more, sleep, and visit the group children's home where I currently work. They all look forward to Sparky's visits. His favorite resident is Jimmy, mainly because Jimmy caters to Sparky's first and second favorite things to do in life.

I believe it was fate and not a weird coincidence that all the one-eyed Sparkies were in our care. All of them have been very special to us. I think we were special to them too. The two Sparkies that I knew taught me caring, devotion, and how to share love. They were a constant in my life, and I am much enriched by the experience.

I find it both curious and puzzling that our family was blessed with raising three one-eyed Sparkies. It had to be fate. Someone or something meant for us to look after them. I think the reason was far beyond the protection, safety, and love we gave to them. Yes, it was fate.

Jeannette S.

Pettrucio

Even though Pettrucio was not my dog, I had a most unusual experience with this poodle.

I lived in my current house as a child with my mother, father, and two brothers and sisters. Later in 1979, after my parents divorced, my mother moved us into another home that we owned. We lived here for several years and then moved on.

Several years later, my father remarried, and his new wife owned Pettrucio. They lived for some time in the house where I now live. It was here that Pettrucio was buried. He was quite old and had lost most of his fur and his eyesight. Eventually, he died from a heart attack.

He must have had a great attachment to this house as he still remains here. His nails can be heard clicking on the floors as he patrols the house at night.

I have also seen him a couple of times. One day as I was standing at the kitchen sink washing dishes, I happened to look around and saw him. I was startled as his nails hadn't made their usual noise on the floor, and I hadn't expected him. I looked back again seconds later, and he was gone.

I wasn't even thinking of him at that time. I wasn't important in his life, and as I said, I didn't know him. Pettrucio must be waiting for his mistress to return for him.

He died about 20 years ago, and I can only assume that he is looking for his beloved owner. If true, it says a lot about the type of loyalty a pet can have for his owner. Pets could teach us a lot about love and loyalty, if we would only listen.

I would feel fortunate to have a pet who showed such devotion. Pettrucio's continued search should inspire us all to be kinder and more loving.

Carol A. Stephanski-Horton

Precious Cat, AKA PC & Peekers

PC lived down the street from my parents. He visited them every day, so my parents finally started to feed him. My folks felt PC didn't want to compete for attention with the many children and dogs who shared his home. Many months went by, and my dad finally went to our neighbor's home to ask if he might keep PC, as he was with him most all the time anyway. They readily agreed. Peekers, as my dad usually called him, never went back to his original home, even though he was free to go. It was evident that he chose my dad, so that's the way it turned out.

My folks took a walk each night, and PC went along with them. He stayed at their side just as a dog would. He never ventured any further away and remained at their side.

They had to move out of state and felt PC, or Peekers, would do best if he stayed with us. We loved him already and were eager to have him.

He continued to enjoy his nightly walks with me as he had with my folks. He followed my daughter to school one day, even though she told him to go home. She phoned me from school to alert me to come for him. By the time I arrived, he had already left. PC was in an area that was strange to him and got lost. He got about six blocks away from home, and a neighbor called me. He was really glad to see me.

He was so dear to us. We pampered him occasionally with his favorite people food of broccoli, cantaloupe or chicken livers. Whenever he smelled any of those foods, he would run to the kitchen and would beg for them until he was rewarded with his favorites.

PC never showed an interest in toys. We had a big gray bunny, named Holly, who was a close friend and companion for PC. Holly was about the same size as PC, and they each weighed about 12 pounds. He would sit and clean Holly's ears for her, and she sat there peacefully and let him. It was apparent they really had a close relationship.

When any of our family members were not feeling well, PC would sleep on that person's bed that night. When he felt they had recovered, he slept in his usual place on my bed.

When he reached the age of nine, he became ill, though we were unaware at the time. About a week before he died, I had a very vivid dream. PC was in my daughter's arms, standing beneath an archway. She was crying and waving good-bye with PC's little paw. I could not make my way to them. When I awakened, I was very confused and upset. PC was asleep next to me, as per usual, and seemed fine.

A week later, he became very ill and could hardly walk. I immediately took him to the vet. He was diagnosed with a formidable disease and would die very soon. We agreed he should not suffer. I was distraught and did not want PC to sense my anxiety and make him more anxious. As I was walking to the front office to pay for the services, I looked back and saw my daughter holding PC in her arms, crying, and waving good-bye to me with his little paw. She was standing under a curved archway. It was the exact, same thing I had seen a week before in my dream. The memory came flooding back to me, and I was so freaked out, I had to leave the building.

Perhaps, PC was preparing me or warning me that it was his time to go. We miss him terribly. It is so hard to let a family member go.

Robin Loggans

Joey

My new little Guinea Pig, Joey, and I had a lot of leisure time to get acquainted, as I was on sick leave for nine weeks. He proved to be a delight.

He liked to lie on my stomach and be petted or combed. He voiced his pleasure by making little cooing sounds throughout the whole process.

He was a good game player and would also mimic movements that I made. If I hopped my hand toward him, he would also hop and make little squeals of delight, then run in circles.

One of his favorite games was his version of football. He would pick up a writing pen, run in circles, and then throw it on the floor. When I picked it up and placed it back on the desk, Joey would repeat his maneuvers again. This continued as long as I would go along with it. I hadn't expected as much activity from a Guinea Pig and found that he proved to be a devoted pet. He enjoyed any social activity and even made friends with the two dogs who were eventually added to the family.

The first dog, Murphy, did scare Joey one time. Murphy smelled Joey, and he might have thought Murphy was going to taste him instead of give him a kiss. There was a close call one time, when a guest came over with her dog who immediately tried to eat him. The dog was never invited back.

A terrible weekend in 1994, Murphy became terribly ill. Much attention was given to her in order for her to survive. At this time, Joey was seven years old, which is pretty old for a Guinea Pig. One morning I came downstairs and gave Joey fresh food then returned upstairs to care for Murphy.

Later that day, I saw that Joey hadn't touched his food. Much to my horror, on close examination I noticed he had died sometime during the night. I felt badly, as I didn't know he wasn't feeling well, and I was upset that I hadn't been there for him when he needed me. Joey was cremated, and he is still with us.

For several days after Joey died, I heard him make all the little sounds he used to make when he was happy or excited. I feel he wanted to assure me that he was OK and needed to check on us to make sure that we were also. I was grateful to have had another opportunity to be near him.

Sue Stange

Missy

Missy proved to be one of the most faithful and affectionate dogs in my life. She was a black Dachshund and Cocker Spaniel mix. My heart ached for her when I realized that she had been abused. If anyone held a newspaper or a fly swatter, she would cringe and disappear immediately. She was probably about two years old when she came to live with us in 1981, and I can't imagine why anyone would mistreat such a loving animal.

Missy seemed to be happy, and she adored my family. She made it her job to oversee our property and warn us if anyone trespassed.

For several years, she was very energetic and healthy, but eventually, kidney disease became a problem. She was able to function quite well on prescription dog food for a long time. Eventually, the disease worsened, and I gave her subcutaneous fluids (injected under the skin) at home each day.

One night I returned from work around midnight and found her in a bad way. She came to me and stared into my eyes with love and devotion expressed on her face. Missy then walked to my mother and looked at her in the same manner. I did what I could to make her comfortable. I realized that the time had come to ease her suffering.

The next morning, as I rushed her to the vet's office, she died in my arms on the way. Perhaps, she was aware the night before that she would be leaving us very soon, and she was saying her good-byes when she came to us with such a heartfelt expression.

It was so difficult to go through the grief we felt. I longed to have her back again and have everything as it was before. Her stay with us, of nine years, was much too short.

When her condition worsened this last time, I knew I might not have her with me much longer, but I tried to keep a positive attitude. She had rallied many times before.

For several days after her death, I heard her toenails clicking down the hall. She must have been making her rounds to see if we were safe and to protect her property. When I told my mother that I had heard Missy walking down the hall, she said that she had also. It reinforced my belief that Missy lingered behind to give us the comfort we needed. It also helped me accept the fact that she was with us in spirit. This comforted me.

C. C.

Fat Cat

You just read about my pet Missy, and now I would like you to hear the story of my cat, Fat Cat.

The name isn't very glamorous, but I called her that with much affection. Her gray and cream body was a bit round; thus, the name.

Someone had tossed her out, and she was wandering up and down the street and looked so forlorn. My heart went out to her.

When she reached our house, I asked my mother if I could take her in. I was in high school and was a responsible person. Mom told me no! She didn't do that often. Not too long before Fat Cat came by, we had lost one of our pets in a tragic accident, and my mom wasn't ready for another pet.

I must confess that I would sneak out of the house to feed Fat Cat, and my mom didn't know about it. Fat Cat stayed around the yard, of course, enjoying the handouts. Eventually, Mom fell in love with her as well, and Fat Cat moved inside.

We were good for each other. Eventually, we were able to read each other's thoughts. She also read my body language very well. When I didn't feel well, she spent all her time on the bed with me. She was an excellent nurse. If I left the room, she followed along.

For 16 years, we were the best of friends and confidants to the end. Fat Cat's last three years were difficult. She had some type of autoimmune disease and had to have her platelet count monitored often to determine the amount of steroids she needed. She tolerated the treatments very well.

The next problem was a rare eye disease. She was taken to several specialists. It was finally agreed that she would be more comfortable if the more seriously affected eye was removed. Trouper that she was, she adjusted to this operation after a short while.

Soon after the surgery, she developed a pressure sore at the heel of a back foot. I did a lot of research to help it heal over. That was not the end of her problems. Diabetes had to rear its ugly head. Fat Cat was such a dear. She had insulin shots twice a day. I think she knew that all the things I did were to help her. Her special diet helped to control the diabetes for quite some time. It was not uncommon for me to sit up all through the night with her at her worst times. Other times I set the alarm so I could check on her during the night. Eventually, Fat Cat reached the point where she would wake me up when she wanted to eat or use the litter box. They were there for her, but I think she was reassured when I helped her. I was more than pleased to do so. She trusted me completely. She was always there for me when I was sick, and I gladly returned the favor. We needed each other.

Her last problem was renal failure. It progressed rapidly. It was time for her to leave me. I held her in my arms to comfort her as she was put in her final sleep.

It is now a year later, and I still get a glimpse of her walking across the bedroom. It is ever so brief, but enough to reassure me. Her spirit remains here also. Maybe as long as I need her to be.

C. C.

Angel

It is very traumatic when a beloved pet dies. Angel was the third of my pets to die. Missy, Fat Cat, and Angel were very dear to me.

I was able to have Angel in my care and heart for seven years. When she was diagnosed with a terminal illness, I knew it was her time to go. I held her closely and stroked her when she entered her final sleep.

A short time after her death, I began to see just a glimpse of her from time to time. She was there – only for a moment, but it was enough to help me through my grief.

C. C.

156

Toby

Toby was a blonde Persian cat and a really loving animal. He came to me when he was six years old. He originally came from a pet store, and then he went from roommate, to roommate, to me. I think of him as my "used" cat, as he had been with two other owners.

He was an indoor pet, but one day he just decided to run away from home. I was devastated, and my major concern was how would he deal with traffic, noise, other animals, and the lack of food? He still belonged to my roommate at that time, but I was the one who searched for him. I did the usual things to try to locate him. For two months, I remained in contact with the Humane Society, rang doorbells, and posted notices in the area. Each day I became more concerned that I might not see him again. Meanwhile, his owner just went out and got another cat.

Toby must have decided, he didn't like it on his own. One day he just showed up at the door as if to say, "Hi Honey, I'm home." Of course, I was relieved, "forgave" him, and welcomed him home. I claimed him as mine, which was fine with his former owner. She said, "He always loved you best anyway."

Time seems to have passed so quickly. I was so used to him greeting me when I came home, spending quiet time on the bed in the evenings, and sharing so many nice times together.

Then it happened. His sudden illness was quickly followed by his death on July 13, 1988. I felt cheated that we didn't have more time to be together. For several weeks, my one litany was, "I just want to hold him one more time."

Two months later, I had a powerful dream in which I had a phone call from the vet. He told me that if I came right away, I could see Toby, but I had to hurry. I started out immediately. The trip took me through dangerous swamps, a jungle, and then mountains. After I fought my way through those obstacles, I faced a final steep mountain that had to be climbed. It was a very hard journey, and it left me with little energy. Finally, I reached Toby, and I held him for one long and last time. I got my wish.

It was a few weeks later that I had another both real and powerful dream. In it I went to my parent's home and saw Toby playing in the yard with Red, my dog who died in 1972. They appeared to be happy and enjoying their games. Red ran up to me, put her paws on my shoulders, licked my face, and ran back to play with Toby. I went inside for a short while. When I returned to the yard, I called out to Toby and told him it was time to go home. He didn't come — he just stood there, but Red came to give me another lick on the face. He ran back to Toby, and the two of them ran off into the distance, still playing games, and acting happy just to be together. The dream was so profound that the next morning I knew Red and Toby were together. They had found each other and would never be alone.

I don't think our animals really leave us. I think we tune them out. I am very aware of my animal's emotions. I have seen far too often, people don't recognize that their fur-faced children have emotions much like our own. I have seen them in sadness and when they show happiness as well as loss. They grieve much the same as we do. Pets definitely mourn the loss of another pet or person.

When Toby died, there was an emptiness in the house. I feel now that his spirit is here, and that comforts me. I must be satisfied with that.

Dorothy Ann

Sally

Sally was born October 28, 1971. She passed into Grace March 9, 1985.

She was a lovely Blue Point Siamese with eyes the color of turquoise stones. She was eight weeks old when I got her. We had more than 13 years together, but I wish it could have been longer. We crammed a lot of love into the time we had together.

She used to love racing down the hall and going for a long slide on the throw rug. She invented this game. It was her very own Playland, and this was her favorite ride. Her second-best fun thing to do was to throw a toy from the top of the stairs, race down to fetch it, and do it all over again.

She had as much curiosity as energy. She learned to open doors very early in life, be it the bathroom door (I think she liked the squeak) or the hutch doors in the dining room. Sally never bothered the things inside the hutch, but like all cats she was aware when something was out of place. I think she was pretty much a neatnik.

Each morning, we shared breakfast. She would sit on a chair beside me at the table. Buttered toast was a favorite, but corn on the cob was special to her. She had a unique way of nibbling and was most fastidious as she circled the cob.

When my son was a baby, she slept at the foot of his crib and watched over him. She seemed to know that she was guarding a precious baby.

It has been 15 years since she made her journey home. I miss her each day, but I know her spirit is here. We still hear her running down the hall. I suspect she is enjoying a slide on the throw rug. She seems to have retained her old energy level, and it is serving her well.

Dorothy

Dusty Lynne

Dusty came to us at the age of nine from a family who, I suspect, did not give her the best of care. My husband and I made sure that she would feel secure and safe with us. She was a gorgeous Seal Point Siamese as was our other cat, Boots. They became inseparable. Dusty was totally smitten with Boots. She would chase after him, jump on him, lick his face, and give him a tender bite on the neck that he would return in kind. He pretended to dislike it, but I think he secretly enjoyed it and was a lover himself. Sometimes, she would chase after us and attack our legs, or she would gently and playfully nip at our feet.

She loved to hide. When my friend, Susie, came to visit, Dusty would hide in her handbag. Of course, she was found out before Susie left with her. She would also honor Susie by rolling over on her back, inviting her to rub her belly. Another good place to hide was in my coat sleeve. She would work her way up, until she couldn't be seen. She must have felt secure in dark, warm places.

Dusty knew she was very special to my husband, and each morning she asked him for breakfast. Of course, he followed her orders.

We were in bed one evening with the lights out and ready to fall asleep when Dusty decided it was playtime. She had a toy and was throwing it up in the air near the bed. I told my husband that she wanted to play, but he just fell asleep. It must have been a fun game, and she spent quite a long time at it. I finally fell asleep after Dusty curled up in my arms. Next morning, when I made the bed, I found her "toy" where she had carefully placed it, under the blanket on my husband's side of the bed. I yelled out, and he came running. He saw the mouse exactly where she had placed it. My husband had a laugh and praised her for her good deed. She earned a chicken dinner later that night.

She was very brave. Dusty went through a long illness and tolerated her treatments without protest. Unfortunately, we did not get the happy ending we prayed for. Our grief was overwhelming. It only helped a bit to remember her and her favorite games and antics. We had no choice but to settle for our memories.

Dusty had a unique voice. After her death, I realized the tone of the clock chime was very similar to her voice. At times, I feel she is speaking to me when it chimes.

At times, I think Boots is aware of her presence. He seems to listen, put his ears back, and investigates smells on the floor. I suspect he is aware of both Sally, my Siamese cat who died years ago, and Dusty. Many mornings, he acts as though they are chasing him down the hallway. He'll stop quickly, as though to let them catch up, then run again. I can tell by his posture and movements that he also dreams of wrestling and playing with Dusty.

Yes, my angel-babies are still here, and I am pleased that they can still enjoy their loving home. I feel they come to us every day. I hope in time, I will be able to accept that God needed another angel to sing in His kingdom.

Dorothy

Positive Steps to Help Deal With Grief

Now that he is gone, what do I do? There are support groups for those who have lost a beloved pet. Ask your local SPCA if they have a support group. If none are available, form one. If you have a computer, check the message boards. Do a search for "grief AND pet loss." You will be able to locate many others who are going through the same pain and will be eager to "talk" with you. If you or a friend don't have a computer, your local library does. Check the library for a book dealing with grief for a lost pet.

Some excellent places concerning grief on the Web are...

Veterinary Information Network / Pet Care Forum / Pet Loss / Animal Issues Web site at www.vin.com/PetCare/Series/PetLoss.htm. They have a message board, a list of recommended books, and other Web links concerning grief.

- Superdog's Pet Loss pages at www.superdog.com/petloss.htm. They also have links to pet-loss counselors, books, cemeteries, urn markers, dedications, and a list of worthy animal causes to which you can donate.

- Lightning Strike Pet Loss Support pages "offering a 'cybershoulder' for grieving pet owners" at www.lightning-strike.com/frame_pet-loss.htm. They have a chat room, message board, book links, Web links, and much more.

Express your grief in the same manner you would if a family member died. Cry, sob, and talk about your beloved pet. When a human family member dies, there is much support from others. You have ample opportunities to talk about the deceased. Your pet was a family member too.

Ask your friends and family to help you through this period. You may have to tell them that your need to talk about your pet is important to you.

Write a letter to your pet, and tell him how you are feeling right now. Tell him how much he enriched your life. Make a list of all his actions that made you laugh or smile, the special things that happened to the two of you, and how much his love meant to you. Pour your heart out. Keep the letter, and read it again when most of the sadness has eased.

Gather the photographs and other mementos you may have, and create a photo album or scrapbook of you and your pet's life together.

Plan something in his honor. It might be a tree planted in his favorite place in the yard or a piece of garden statuary that honors him. Perhaps, your city would like a special tree or bench donated to the local park to honor him.

There are many animal charities and rescue groups that would enjoy and value your help. You might volunteer at a local shelter. Ask others to help you raise funds for animals in need.

If you have thought of taking another animal into your home, visit your local animal shelter. Consider an animal with special needs, an older animal or one who has spent their allotted time and is scheduled to be euthanized. If you already have a pet, take it with you, and let him or her choose a companion. That way they are more apt to be compatible. You just might find another Arf Angel or Heavenly Creature.

Animals who are outgoing and social would appreciate the company of another when left at home. If you work, you can also consider daycare for your animal.

If you are unable to adopt at this time, you or a family member might consider being a volunteer at a shelter a few hours a week. The need is great for someone to walk the dogs, socialize and interact with the animals, feed them, clean cages or pens, and just stroke or talk to them. Volunteers who groom animals also help them look their best and increase their chances for adoption. The most important thing is to find loving homes for all those in need.

There are times when shelters need foster homes on a temporary basis. It is such a good feeling to hand raise orphaned animals or watch over a mother and her litter until the babies reach an adoptable age. You can make a big difference with any small gesture.

Some groups now have Web sites to list animals available for adoption and what the group needs in the way of donations of goods and services. If you are unable to commit to a set schedule, perhaps, you can volunteer to work on a shelter's Web site or help them create one. (See Petfinder's offer of help mentioned later in this chapter.) If you are a photographer and have a digital camera, you can take appealing photographs to post on the Web site, or create flyers to distribute in your area. You can collect blankets and supplies to be used at the shelter. You can visit a local shelter, then organize a group to locate homes for all the "inmates."

Would your pet expect you to share your home with another? He probably knows you have enough love to give to another pet. One woman wrote that she immediately gets another animal. It helps her get through her grief and provides a home for another animal in need.

You may not want another pet because you don't want to experience the sadness of loss again. I felt that way for quite some time. I'm sorry that I waited. There was a hole in my heart and an emptiness in my life that only another pet could fill.

If you feel you are ready for a new scaled, feathered or furry family member, again, the Web is a great place to start. We adopted Annie (Orphan Annie Warbucks-Perry, nee Hyacinth), a longhaired Chihuahua mix, from the Bill Foundation. This organization rescues animals and then finds homes for them. They work with the Los Angeles City and County shelters. Their Web site can be found at www.billfoundation.org.

We found Annie through the Bill Foundation at another Web site called Petfinder. They have a great database and search engine for finding a pet and the many rescue groups and shelters that offer them. It's at www.petfinder.org. They also offer to add a Web page, with any shelter or rescue group's information, to their Web site. This way any group can list animals available for adoption and have a Web presence – free!

Again, The Pet Care Forum, at www.vin.com/PetCare, is a valuable, general-information resource. It covers almost all animal issues and is aimed at the lay person, not just veterinarians. There are several categories of message boards, chats, a library, articles concerning health, behavior, selecting the right type of animal for you, and an opportunity to ask the staff veterinarians questions.

Each person grieves differently. Only you know what is best for you. Whatever works for you, act on it.

Here's hoping that this book with it's stories, suggestions, and information have been helpful to you. I hope you feel less alone in your loss. Write to me, and tell me what helped you get through the pain of your loss. Sharing usually helps.

In Closing

A portion of my profit from the sale of *Arf Angels and Other Heavenly Creatures* will be donated to animal shelters and nonprofit organizations who save and care for animals.

Over the past years, I have gained so much from the animals who (yes, I mean who!) have shared my life. Money earned from the sale of *Arf Angels* can benefit animals in need.

It has been three years since Barney left. I feel he helped me evolve into a better person. I really didn't think that I would have another pet, but now we have three. Molly, a cat, was left behind when a person in the neighborhood moved away. The poor baby had to fend for herself for several months before I learned about her.

When she came into our yard, I reached down to pet her. She was starved for both attention and food. If I stopped petting her, she stood on her hind legs to reach my hand and ask for more. She continued to do this as I made my way into the house. She hasn't been outside since.

After Molly was here for a few months, I decided to look for a dog. That's how Annie came into my life. She is a 13-pound Chihuahua mix. She came from the Bill Foundation, mentioned in the previous chapter. Annie is very affectionate and demands very little attention, but she gets a lot. This dear little one, whose eyes are those of an old soul, will do anything to go for a walk or ride in the car. The longer she is here, the more endearing she becomes. I often wonder how I ever managed without her.

Sophie is the third. You may have guessed that Susan brought her home. She found her in a nearby city, and she appeared to have been living on her own for a couple of months. She hadn't fared very well, as she was starved and too ill to stand. It took two surgeries and much medication to return her to reasonable health. For about a two-month period it was necessary that she be held during the day, and I slept with a hand on her, so I could feel if she moved at night.

Sometimes I wonder if Barney was responsible for her coming into my life. Maybe, I haven't evolved as much as he expected, and he recruited Sophie to complete the job. I think she is here to teach me to be more patient. Again! I feel I am a pretty laid back person, but Sophie begs to differ. She is now a sassy little thing and is the first pet I have ever had who talks. She whines, moans, and makes unusual little guttural sounds. I swear that she talks in complete sentences. Many times, I've thought I've heard Susan calling me when it actually was Sophie. She tells me when her food is to be in her bowl, when to take a break, and when to go to bed. She expects me to have lights out by 10:15 p.m. If I don't, she will talk in such a loud manner that I can't hear the dialog on the television. This little 10-pound fur-ball has crept deeply into my heart.

I don't think my life could be any better.

Do you have a pet-related story you would like to share with others? I am interested in stories involving your pet that can be published and are unique, inspirational, contain premonitions of impending events, after death visits, brave actions by your pet, and life changing experiences. Don't be afraid to include details that show emotional involvement or events. These stories may help others who are dealing with difficult or similar circumstances. I may include stories about heroic and giving people too. The subject may be living or dead. Perhaps there will be enough for a new book and raise more money for animal causes. Please enclose permission to use your story along with photos (if possible), contact information, and how you want your name signed. You can play your part in helping animal causes and provide a good read for others too.

Best wishes to all of you and yours. May there be many "Arf Angels" and other "Heavenly Creatures" in your future. In other words ... I wish you an abundance of love in your life.

I would enjoy hearing from any reader who may have a comment, a question or a story to relate. Please send them to:

Anita Perry/Arf Angels
P.O. Box 2982
Castro Valley, Ca. 94546

Or e-mail them to Anita@ArfAngels.net.

You're welcome to visit ArfAngels.net, and see what's new, at any time.

Animal groups who wish to use this book as a fundraiser
may purchase it at a discount at
ArfAngels.net.

About the Author

Anita Perry combined her love of writing and her compassion for animals to produce a book that is sometimes humorous, sometimes sad. She has owned, rescued, fostered, learned from, and loved many animals in her life. One of those animals was her dog, Barney, who started the ball rolling by making his presence known after his death. Over two years of research went into gathering many compelling stories of animals returning to their caretakers.

Ms. Perry is a freelance writer and was a columnist for San Francisco Bay Area newspapers. She wrote a monthly garden column and other local interest articles.

Lightning Source UK Ltd.
Milton Keynes UK
UKOW05f2143191113

221454UK00001B/38/A